DIVORCE GUIDE FOR WASHINGTON

Mark Patterson, Attorney

Self-Counsel Press Inc.
a subsidiary of
International Self-Counsel Press Ltd.

Printed in Canada

First edition: July 1977
Second edition: 1980
Third edition: 1983
Fourth edition: 1987
Fifth edition: 1989
Sixth edition: 1990; Reprinted: 1991
Seventh edition: 1991
Eighth edition: 1992; Reprinted: 1992; 1993; 1994
Ninth edition: 1994; Reprinted: 1994; 1995; 1996
Tenth edition: 1998; Reprinted: 1998; 2000
Eleventh edition: 2002

Cataloging in Publication Data

Patterson, Mark T.
    Divorce guide for Washington

    (Self-counsel legal series)
    ISBN 1-55180-389-5

    1. Divorce—Law and legislation—Washington (State)—Popular works
    2. Divorce—Law and legislation—Washington (State)—Forms.
    I. Title. II. Series
    KFW100.Z9D35 2002   346.79701'66   C2002-910444-0

Self-Counsel Press Inc.
a subsidiary of
International Self-Counsel Press Ltd.

1704 N. State Street   1481 Charlotte Road
Bellingham, WA 98225   North Vancouver, BC V7J 1H1
USA   Canada

CONTENTS

TABLE

SAMPLES

DO-IT-YOURSELF DIVORCE FORMS
AVAILABLE FROM THE PUBLISHER

If, after reading this book, you decide to go ahead with your divorce without the help of a lawyer, you may want to purchase the package of forms that can be used in conjunction with this guide. But remember, if your spouse contests your divorce, you must consult a lawyer.

Divorce Forms for Washington are available where you bought this book or from the publisher.

In some cases, you will need to photocopy the forms *after* completing them but *before* signing them. Again, read the guide thoroughly.

The kit contains one copy of the following forms:

Confidential Information Form (DRPSCU 09.0200)

Addendum to Confidential Information Form (DRPSCU 09.0210)

Sealed Financial Source Documents (DRSCU 09.0220)

Petition for Dissolution of Marriage (DR 01.0100

Summons (DR 01.0200)

Return of Service (DR 01.0250)

Acceptance of Service (DR 01.0310)

Joinder (DR 01.0330)

Financial Declaration (DR 01.0550)

Motion and Declaration for Default (DR 03.0100)

Order of Default (DR 03.0200)

Note for Dissolution Calendar (DR 03.0300)

Temporary Order (DR 04.0250)

Findings of Fact and Conclusions of Law (DR 04.0300)

Decree (DR 04.0400)

Declaration for Service by Publication (DR 01.0260)

Order for Service by Publication (DR 01.0265)

Summons by Publication (DR 01.0270)

Motion and Declaration to Serve by Mail (DR 01.0280)

Order Allowing Service by Mail (DR 01.0285)

Summons by Mail (DR 01.0290)

Waiver of Rights Under Soldiers and Sailors' Civil Relief Act and Admission of Service

Washington Child Support Schedule Instructions for Worksheets

Washington State Child Support Schedule Worksheets

Parenting Plan (DR 01.0400)

Order of Child Support (DR 01.0500)

Motion and Declaration for Temporary Order (DR 04.0100)

Declaration in Support of Parenting Plan (DR 04.0120)

Motion/Declaration for Ex Parte Restraining Order (DR 04.0150)

Ex Parte Restraining Order (DR 04.0170)

To obtain the package of *Divorce Forms,* please complete and mail in the form below.

✂--

To:

SELF-COUNSEL PRESS
1704 N. State Street
Bellingham, Washington 98225
Please send *Divorce Forms for Washington*

_____ sets of *Divorce Forms* at $15.95 each	_____
Sales tax of 7.8%	_____
Plus postage and handling	__$3.50__
Total:	_____

❑ Enclosed is a money order for $ _____ which is payment in full.

OR

❑ I would like to charge this purchase to my credit card:

❑ Visa/MasterCard account number: _____

❑ Expiry date: _____

❑ Signature: _____

I understand that no legal advice can be given with these forms.

Name: _____

Address: _____

City: _____

State: _____ Zip code: _____

Telephone: _____

Note: Prices are subject to change without notice.

NOTICE TO READERS

Laws are constantly changing. Every effort is made to keep this publication as current as possible. However, neither the author nor the publisher can accept any responsibility for changes to the law or practice that occur after the printing of this publication. Please be sure that you have the most recent edition.

Note: The fees quoted in this book are correct at the time of publication. However, fees are subject to change without notice. For current fees, please check with the court registry nearest you.

INTRODUCTION

This book, written by a lawyer, is directed toward filling the general public's need for information. Every citizen should know his or her rights and know how to use the courts to enforce these rights. This book is just one in the Self-Counsel Legal Series.

The directions and explanations in this book are reduced to a simple step-by-step process to help you understand the divorce proceedings.

You can obtain your own divorce, as it is the right of every citizen to take his or her own case to court. It will require time and energy on your part, but the ultimate objective of this book is to make lack of money no obstacle to obtaining a divorce. Your efforts could save you as much as $600 in lawyer's fees. Even if you are completely unfamiliar with the operation of the law and the courts, you should be able to obtain a divorce for as little as $200 provided there is no disagreement over custody and you are prepared to represent yourself in court.

However, there are some situations in which this book cannot help you and, in these cases, *consultation with a lawyer is absolutely mandatory.* Specifically, if your divorce is contested *for any reason whatsoever,* you will require a lawyer. If you cannot afford a lawyer, you should consult your local legal aid office. According to past statistics, contested divorces account for only 15 percent of the total number; this book is for the other 85 percent.

1
CAN I DO MY OWN DIVORCE?

a. DO I NEED A LAWYER?

There are cases in which you cannot help yourself and will need advice. Even if your divorce is uncontested, there may be procedural complications in your case that will require the services of a lawyer. For example, if you have no idea where your spouse is residing you will have trouble serving the documents on him or her.

As well, there may be maintenance payments, child custody, support and visitation (or parenting functions, as the court now prefers to call them), and matrimonial property matters to be negotiated. If you and your spouse cannot agree on some of these issues, you may want to retain the services of a lawyer to negotiate them.

If you find yourself in these circumstances, you should obtain an estimate of fees for the work to be done. If you are not happy with the cost quoted, feel free to "shop around."

Contrary to popular opinion, most lawyers will give you a quote based on the handling of the case in court, or, for that matter, for any other particular problem for which you feel you need a lawyer. Many people are embarrassed to ask a lawyer for the price of his or her services, especially in family and divorce matters. This can be a costly mistake. DON'T MAKE IT!

The actual court presentation causes the layperson the greatest confusion and fear. If you are uncomfortable at the thought of appearing in court by yourself, you should consider retaining a lawyer for this purpose only.

If you decide to do everything yourself, you should be aware that, while most judges are very cooperative, some are not. Therefore, you should carefully read the section on the court hearing and attend a court session before the same judge prior to your hearing. This will acquaint you with the particular judge's manner of handling divorce cases.

If you do everything yourself, including the court appearance, your divorce could cost you less than $200. You must pay a filing fee to the county clerk. It is now $120, but is changed often by the state legislature, so you should call the county clerk to find out the correct amount. If you must serve copies of the papers on your spouse, the cost of service will probably be between $20 and $30. Once again, you should call the county sheriff or a process server in the county in which your spouse lives for an estimate of cost.

A 1971 United States Supreme Court decision held that a person sincerely seeking a divorce does not have to pay the filing fee if to do so would be a hardship. If you cannot afford the filing fee or cost of service and you want to take advantage of this decision, you should fill in a form entitled In Forma Pauperis, and the court will order the county clerk to file your papers without the fee (see chapter 5).

Even if you have no intention of "doing it yourself," this book should serve as a useful "pre-lawyer" guide to what is happening in your divorce case. It will enable you to be better prepared when seeing your lawyer and to follow your divorce through step by step. This alone should save you unnecessary legal fees.

b. THINK BEFORE YOU START

Think twice about everything that you are doing. Be fully aware of the consequences of your decision to bring a divorce action but particularly what the position of you, your spouse, and your children will be as a result. Seek help from a marriage counselor or other qualified person if you feel there is any chance of a reconciliation.

If you are determined to proceed with a divorce, follow all the suggested procedures very carefully. They are all important. Likewise, all forms must be completed with meticulous attention to detail. If you do sloppy work, you could end up paying a lawyer twice as much to correct your mistakes. Be methodical and well prepared at all times.

Be persistent. Do not be afraid to ask questions about the law, even though there may be people who try to discourage your inquiries. Your sincerity and politeness will encourage the proper responses. Contrary to what you might have heard, the divorce courts are quite efficient. Let's keep them that way by not clogging the process with papers and pleadings that are defective.

Although the employees in the county clerk's office cannot give you legal advice, they can tell you how your papers will be processed through their office and how you can have your case placed on the divorce calendar. You can ask them to show you court files of divorce cases in which a person was self-represented. These court files can show you how to be successful in obtaining your own divorce.

If you are well prepared, you should not have to spend more than a few minutes in the courtroom before a judge. If the judge detects carelessness, you could be in for a bad experience, and your lack of knowledge of courtroom procedure will not help the situation.

If you intend to represent yourself in court, you must be especially well prepared. The judge is not there to block your efforts to obtain a divorce, and in most cases, will be helpful. However, the judge does have a specific job to do and must be satisfied that the requirements of the Marriage Dissolution Act have been complied with. This book provides an outline of the types of questions that will be asked. However, you should attend *at least* one court session of uncontested divorces to familiarize yourself with the conduct of a divorce hearing.

If you find yourself getting in over your head, you will have to make a decision —

(a) to consult a lawyer, or

(b) to drop the action.

The choice is an entirely personal one but, in any event, do not proceed if you do not have a clear understanding of what you are doing. The consequences of errors can be serious and permanent.

c. HOW CAN THIS BOOK HELP ME?

This book is divided into two basic parts. The first part outlines the substantive law of a divorce action. The second part deals with the step-by-step procedure leading up to your court hearing.

In Washington state, a dissolution of marriage (divorce) may be obtained on the ground that the marriage has "irretrievably broken." While the courts encourage reconciliation, the court is not interested in fault-finding and is more interested in the arrangement you and your spouse have decided upon about your family matters.

You and your spouse must carefully decide what you want the court to do about matters such as child support, custody and visitation (that is, parenting functions), and matrimonial debts and property. You must be sure that what is contained in your divorce papers is exactly the form of relief you want and that you have expressed yourself clearly.

The first part of this book should help you focus on these matters.

The second part of this book is where you will find step-by-step procedures. Directions are set out for the start of your action, through all stages, to the completed divorce.

Each of the steps outlined is important, and each one must be completed before proceeding on to the next. Failure to do this will only result in a great deal of delay and confusion at a later stage.

Do not allow technical words to confuse you. If you encounter terms or phrases foreign to you, look them up in a legal dictionary, which can be found at any library. A glossary of the most common terms is provided in this book. Keep a notebook of such information. It will pay you to research your divorce carefully. Again, it is emphasized that ignorance in the early stages could "snowball" into later difficulties.

Throughout the book you will find illustrations of the forms you will need showing how they should be completed. These are included as *samples only* of commonly used sentences and phrases. Do not copy from them word for word. Use them as guides for the general style and form required when you fill out your forms according to your specific situation.

It is not difficult to draft your own clauses. Put a little work into drafting properly structured sentences and, generally, if they state the truth, they will be acceptable.

While you are following the step-by-step procedure, you will find it necessary to refer constantly to these forms. You may not see the reason for some of them, but they are all necessary for the successful completion of your action.

Available from the publisher is a kit of forms to use in the completion of your own divorce (see order form at the front of this book). Fill these forms out, using the samples as guides, and follow the instructions in the book — and you will be well on your way to successfully filing for divorce.

2
WHAT YOU SHOULD KNOW BEFORE YOU BEGIN

a. BASIS OF DIVORCE

Washington legislation uses the word dissolution rather than divorce. You may apply to the court for a dissolution of your marriage on the sole basis that the marriage has irretrievably broken down. The courts are not interested in assigning fault. See the Appendix at the back of this guide for a checklist of steps to take in your divorce proceedings.

b. SEPARATION AGREEMENTS

Once you separate (or even when you are living together but preparing for separation), you and your spouse may want to agree on certain issues such as maintenance and child support, residential provisions for the children, and the division of joint assets. You and your spouse may put this agreement in writing and sign it. This is called a separation agreement.

A separation agreement is a contract between you and your spouse. The court will give this document the same weight as any other contract; therefore, a separation agreement should be given careful consideration. Ideally, a separation agreement should be drawn up by a lawyer and one party should sign in front of that lawyer, the other party in front of a separate lawyer, so that each receives independent advice about the true legal effect of the agreement.

You are not required to have a separation agreement. It is sufficient merely to state what you have agreed upon in your Petition for Dissolution.

If one of the parties was forced to sign the separation agreement, or did not receive independent advice, the court may not acknowledge the agreement. Both you and your spouse should be sure that you understand the terms of the separation agreement and that it says exactly what you want it to say. Changing the terms of a separation agreement is a difficult and costly matter, one that will require the advice of a lawyer.

While it is common for a couple to draw up a binding separation agreement without any legal action being taken, Washington law provides a legal route for setting down the terms of your separation. Once you and your spouse agree to the terms of separation and write a separation agreement, you may have it published in the legal notices section of the newspaper and recorded with the county auditor at the courthouse.

Once the separation agreement is both published and recorded, it is binding on both of you. Keep in mind that even a separation agreement that does not follow this procedure can be binding.

There are many advantages to a separation agreement. Drafting one provides an opportunity to settle your disputes without the cost of litigation. A separation agreement may contain unique clauses that would not have been ordered by the courts, although they may suit your purposes exactly. Therefore, a separation agreement has greater flexibility and potential than a court order.

The provisions of the separation agreement can also be adopted by a judge and made into a formal court order in a divorce action or proceedings in family court, where all the parties are in agreement or where there is no valid reason for having the provisions changed.

If one party attempts to break a separation agreement, the other party should immediately seek the advice of a lawyer, since the issues involved may be numerous and complicated.

Although there is generally no limit to the issues that can be covered in a separation agreement, you and your spouse should give first consideration to the following:

(a) A clause stipulating that neither party will annoy, molest, or interfere with the other

(b) If there are children of the marriage, agreement about the parenting plan (see section d. below)

(c) Maintenance and support for the children, including the amount to be paid and the age to which payments will continue (When discussing this matter with your spouse, you should also consider the requirements of the children beyond high school and, in particular, the question of financial assistance to the children should they wish to go to college.)

(d) Dividing community assets, which may include real property such as stocks, bonds, insurance benefits, and joint income tax returns

(e) If the family home is registered in the joint names of husband and wife, agreement on whether—

  (i) the house should be sold and the proceeds of such sale divided between the parties,

  (ii) one party will buy out the other, or

  (iii) one party will continue to live in the home with the children until the family is grown and out on their own (If the wife is to be the main custodian of the children, it is often agreed that she continue to live in the family home with the children. In this case, definite agreement should be reached on payment of mortgages and major repairs, such as a new roof or new furnace, which might be required from time to time. In addition, you should agree on when the spouse living in the home should pay the other for his or her share of the equity of the home, the amount of that payment, and the rate of interest to be paid on that amount from the date of the agreement to the date of payment.)

(f) If one spouse agrees to pay maintenance to the other, some provision about the amount to be paid, the times of payments, and under what circumstances the payments will cease (e.g., remarriage, the death of either spouse, or the passage of a given number of years)

(g) If there are debts outstanding prior to the separation of the spouses, a clause stating who is responsible for them (Provision should also be made for indemnifying each party against responsibility for debts incurred by the other after the agreement is signed.)

(h) Release of any interest each of you may have against the estate of the other in the event of death

(i) Provision for determining the effective period of the agreement (i.e., whether it is to be an interim agreement to be terminated upon dissolution of the marriage, or whether it is to continue in effect after a divorce decree has been granted) particularly in regard to property settlement, maintenance, and support for children

You may want to look at the example of a separation agreement shown in Sample 1. Remember, this is just one example. Your own situation may differ greatly. Under present law the custody provisions must be contained in the parenting plan Form DR 01.0400, which is shown in Sample 15 in chapter 4.

c. CUSTODY

The state legislature has abolished the use of the words "custody" and "visitation," and has replaced them with the words "parenting functions." Instead of an order or decree granting custody and visitation, each order or decree must contain a "parenting plan" (see Sample 15 in chapter 4).

A parenting plan must contain a decision on whether the major decisions in the child's life will be made jointly, or whether one parent will make the decisions alone (decision making). It must also contain a division of the time that the child will be physically with each parent including provisions for holidays, vacations, and so forth (residential provisions). Finally, the law requires that the parenting plan choose a method of settling disputes between the parents. The method may be mediation, counseling, arbitration, or referral to court action (conflict resolution). In addition to these provisions in which the parties have a choice, there are numerous provisions which must be in every parenting plan.

1. Decision making

The choice you make concerning decision making is about the big decisions such as what school the child will attend, whether non-emergency medical treatment will be given, and what religious training the child will have. The law specifically says that day-to-day decisions will be made by the parent with whom the child is living at the particular time when the problem comes up.

2. Residential provisions

The law does not require any particular division of the child's time. It does require that each plan contain a specific decision on what days the child will spend with each parent. It can provide, for instance, that the child shall reside with the mother during all work days, alternate weekends, and all vacation and holiday time, except those specifically granted to the father, and that the child shall reside with the father every other weekend, every other winter school vacation, the first two weeks of July, and in even-numbered years the following holidays: Christmas Eve, Memorial Day, and Labor Day; and in odd-numbered years, Christmas Day, July 4, and Thanksgiving Day. This is the traditional custody/visitation order. On the other hand, you could go to an equally shared residential time rotating on a month-to-month basis, week-to-week basis, or some other period of time. *Equally shared custody is not favored and can be very harmful to the children. If you decide to do it, you should consult with a lawyer and child psychologist about it before adopting a plan.* The plan may be anywhere in between these examples. There must be some serious danger to the child before a court will eliminate a parent's right to any time of residential care.

3. Conflict resolution

The law requires you to choose a system of deciding disagreements between the parents. The law suggests counseling, mediation, arbitration, or court action. If you have some other agreement, it will probably also be approved. The law also provides an appeal of the decision of the system you have chosen to the superior court. The appeal is to be based on the records kept by the person who decides for you.

d. IF YOU CANNOT AGREE ON A PARENTING PLAN

If you cannot come to an agreement with your spouse on a parenting plan, your only choice is to go to trial (see chapter 4). Before you decide to do that, here are some things you should know about how a judge will decide between your plan and your spouse's plan.

1. Sole decision making

The judge will agree to making one of you the sole decision maker in the following circumstances:

(a) Both parents oppose joint decision making.

(b) One person opposes and the history of the family is that one person has made the decisions regarding the children.

(c) The parents have not demonstrated an ability to cooperate with each other.

(d) The parents live too far apart to communicate with each other quickly enough to make effective decisions.

(e) One parent has abandoned the family for an extended period of time.

(f) One parent has failed or refused, for an extended period of time, to do part or all of the following:

    (i) maintain a loving, stable, consistent, and nurturing relationship with the child;

    (ii) attend to the daily needs of the child, such as feeding, clothing, physical care and grooming, supervision, health care and day care, and engaging in other activities which are appropriate to the development level of the child and that are within the social and economic circumstances of the particular family;

    (iii) attend to adequate education for the child, including remedial or other education essential to the best interests of the child;

    (iv) assist the child in developing and maintaining appropriate interpersonal relationships;

    (v) exercise appropriate judgment regarding the child's welfare, consistent with the child's developmental level and the family's social and economic circumstances.

(g) A parent has a history of physical, sexual, or emotional abuse of the children.

(h) A parent is guilty of serious acts of domestic violence.

2. Dispute resolution

The court will not require you to adopt any form of dispute resolution other than court action if any of items (e) through (h) above are present.

3. Limitations on residential time

The court may limit or otherwise control the time a parent spends with the child by devices such as supervised visitation if —

(a) any of items (e) through (h) above under sole decision making are present,

(b) there is any long-term emotional or physical problem that interferes with the parenting functions described in item (f) under sole decision making above,

(c) there is a lack of emotional ties between parent and child,

(d) abusive conflict is likely to harm the child's psychological growth, or

(e) one parent is withholding access to the child by the other parent for a long time without good cause.

Warning: After the judge has entered a permanent parenting plan as part of your Decree of Dissolution, it is very difficult to change without the agreement of your former spouse. *Be sure to think it through thoroughly and get advice from a child psychologist, attorney, or other person familiar with the problems of divided families before agreeing.*

e. CHILD SUPPORT

A child is entitled to the support of both parents. This right to support cannot be bargained away by the parents through a separate agreement outside of the court. The court will make an order for child support after balancing the needs of the child and the custodial parent with the ability of the non-custodial parent to pay.

The exact amount of child support payments will vary with the circumstances of the parties.

Note: *Child support provisions and parenting plans are revised regularly. To check on changes that might have been introduced since the publication of this book, contact the Office of the Administrator for the Courts, Temple of Justice, P.O. Box 41174, Olympia, 98504-1174 (360) 705-5328.*

The child's basic right to child support payments continues up to the age of majority — 18 years. However, if for health or other justifiable reasons, the child continues to be dependent after the age of 18, the court may order support payments to continue until the child is able to assume independence.

The law requires the courts to use a state-wide child support schedule. The schedule adopted by the legislature is set out in full in Table 1. *Before you calculate child support in your case, check with the county clerk to see if the Child Support Table has been changed.*

Table 1 sets forth the basic child support obligation to be shared by the parents in proportion to their incomes. Sample 2 shows the Child Support Worksheets. The Worksheets provide for basic child support obligations and include additional factors for consideration. They must be completed in each proceeding. Follow the directions on each sheet to determine the correct amount of support. A completed support calculation must be attached to the support order.

If you want to have a support amount either higher or lower than that in the Child Support Table, you must put reasons in your Petition and in your Findings of Fact and Conclusions of Law that will convince the judge that support should be either higher or lower than the obligatory amount. See Sample 3 for definitions and standards for child support.

The Worksheets must be provided to the court if you ask for a temporary order for support on a Motion and Declaration for Temporary Order and the Order of Child Support. They must also be attached to the Decree of Dissolution in every case where there are children involved.

Following the support computation forms are the official instructions that explain how to do the computations (see Sample 4). Be sure that you read the instructions carefully.

The Washington State Legislature requires certain language with regard to wage assignment, which you will find in each of the sample forms in this book. This is *not* optional, and in every divorce decree involving minor children this language *must* be used. In addition, the forms in this book use the mandatory language for medical insurance. This may, however, be changed to increase the requirements of the support obligor. It may not be reduced, however, because under Washington law both parties are required to maintain the children as beneficiaries of any employer-supported medical insurance program.

All support ordered under dissolution decrees must be paid through the state registry unless the parties agree to direct payment and the court approves it as likely to work. These provisions are set out in the support section of the sample decree. *Be sure that all blanks are filled out correctly.*

If child support is needed in your case, you must file, in addition to the other documents, a financial declaration in the required form. (See Sample 23 in chapter 4.)

f. MAINTENANCE FOR A SPOUSE

The court may award maintenance for the spouse under Section 26.09.090 of the Marriage Dissolution Act. In making such an order, the court may consider the following factors:

(a) Whether any amount has been provided to the spouse as custodian of the children of the marriage, if any

(b) The financial resources and obligations of the party seeking maintenance

(c) The cost of re-educating or retraining the spouse seeking maintenance

(d) The duration of the marriage

(e) The standard of living established during the marriage

(f) The physical and emotional conditions of the spouse seeking maintenance

The court will not take into consideration marital misconduct. The court will weigh the needs of the spouse seeking maintenance against the needs and ability to pay of the spouse from whom maintenance is sought.

Maintenance is, in effect, a means of equalizing the incomes of the spouses or former spouses by requiring one to pay the other a monthly amount of money when the court is satisfied that circumstances warrant such equalization.

Maintenance will rarely be granted for a period of longer than one or two years unless the marriage is long term (more than 15 years). The judicial guidelines further state that combined maintenance and child support should never be more than 50 percent of the net income of the paying spouse.

A maintenance order (or an order for child support) may be modified. Where the spouse paying maintenance can show a substantial change of circumstance, he or she may make a petition for modification to the court.

Forms for applying for modifications are available from the Office of the Administrator for the Courts (see section e. above for address).

Maintenance will be discontinued at the death of the spouse paying or the death or remarriage of the spouse receiving maintenance unless prior written agreements or court orders state otherwise.

Once a maintenance order is made by the court, failure to comply may result in a fine or jail term for contempt of court or garnishment of the non-paying spouse's wages or bank account. Note that the court will not generally make a finding of contempt where failure to make maintenance payments is due to a real lack of funds or income on the part of the non-paying spouse.

g. MATRIMONIAL PROPERTY

Under Washington law there are two classes of property: community and separate. Separate property is property owned before marriage, received as a gift or inheritance, or purchased from income earned during a separation. Community property is all property acquired during marriage except gifts or inheritance specifically given to one spouse.

In a divorce action the court has a right to award both classes of property in a way that it determines to be just; however, the normal award is one-half of the community property to each spouse and the separate property to the spouse whose property it is. The division of the property is based on the value of the property, less any amount owed against it.

Factors that lead the court to give more of the property to one spouse than the other are health and earning ability or earning potential. The court usually will not give an unequal division of the property in a marriage of less than 10 to 15 years' duration.

It is important, if you are doing your own divorce, that you and your spouse agree on division of the property. Everything you own must be awarded by the decree or included in your separation agreement. If you and your spouse disagree on division of property or the valuation of the property, you should seek legal counsel.

1. Real property

Matrimonial property matters can be very complicated even if you both agree. If you or your spouse has extensive real estate holdings, you should have a lawyer complete your petition with the correct legal descriptions of the various real estate holdings.

A legal description is the way the court system describes your property. Just as you know your home address, your local court system knows your land by its legal description. If your divorce papers contain incorrect legal descriptions, they will not be legally binding on the property transactions described, and you will have to go through much expense to correct the errors in court.

If you have only your matrimonial home to convey, you may want to do so yourself. In that case, the most accurate way to find out the legal description of your home is to go to the local county courthouse, tell them your address, and ask them to look up your legal description.

You could also employ a title search company (find one in your local *Yellow Pages*) and pay them a nominal fee to search for the legal description at the county assessor's office.

Sometimes the papers you receive when you purchase your home contain the legal description. Be very careful about using this description unless you have checked it with your county assessor's office, since some papers contain small errors.

You must be sure that the legal description in your petition is accurate. Do not hesitate to seek legal advice if you are the least bit confused about your real estate holdings. In such circumstances, the legal advice you receive may save you time and money. The portion of the decree that awards the real estate *must have a complete and accurate legal description*.

2. Personal property

The division of personal property like furniture and the family car is straightforward. But some personal property may be more difficult to divide. The cash value and death benefits of life insurance policies acquired during the marriage are also subject to the community property laws of Washington. You may need to contact your life insurance agent to determine not only the values of any policies, but the most economical way to convert or retain their values.

Most retirement plans earned during the marriage are property to be divided in the dissolution. These are difficult to value, but where the spouse has been in the plan a number of years, particularly if nearing retirement, the plan may well be the most valuable community asset. If one spouse has considerable time in a plan, an accountant or attorney should be consulted about its valuation and division.

13

You and your spouse may also have to decide how to divide any joint income tax refund you may receive. This is also considered personal property. You are still a married person during the 90-day reconciliation period following the filing of your Petition for Dissolution, and you can file a joint return if your tax year ends before the divorce decree is filed. Remember to make provision within your petition for the division of any tax refund or debt that may arise from your last jointly filed income tax return. In this way you can avoid any future dispute.

h. RESTRAINING ORDERS

Court orders can require one spouse to do something in favor of the other, such as to pay child support, release control of the children, and so forth.

Often, these orders may contain specific provisions requiring a spouse to refrain from acts of violence or harassment aimed at the other. These latter provisions are called restraining orders and are often crucial to the protection of a person from serious danger, especially in the period immediately following separation or a major confrontation.

By either acting alone or through a lawyer, you may make a written motion, accompanied by a declaration, seeking a restraining order. The restraint may be the only relief sought, or it may be combined with other matters, such as a temporary distribution of certain property or temporary child support.

The declaration, filed together with the motion, is a statement of facts which justify and support the request for relief. (See Sample 5.)

Commonly, the two types of relief sought by a motion of this kind are —

    (a) immediate relief, such as the restraining provision, which must be granted immediately in order to prevent serious harm or harassment, and

    (b) other relief, such as property distribution or child support, which can wait at least a few days.

The motion may ask that the first type of relief be granted immediately on a temporary basis, and that the opposing spouse be required to appear on a certain date (known as the return date) and "show cause" why that order should not be made permanent, pending the final resolution of the case.

In addition, the order will require the opposing spouse to show cause why the other provision should not also be issued as orders at the time.

Because this order, known as an Order to Show Cause, may be granted without notice to the opposing spouse, the courts are limited as to what kind of relief can be ordered immediately. (See Sample 5.)

Only if you, the moving party, are in actual danger, or under threat of danger, will the order take effect immediately, and then it must be worded so that the only provisions that take effect immediately concern the dangerous situation.

The other provision sought in the motion will take effect after your spouse has been served with the Order to Show Cause and has had a minimum of six court days from the time of receiving the order until the return date, at which time he or she may appear with or without a lawyer to argue against the continuation of the restraining provisions or the issuance of any other relief.

The return date must be stated in the order, so your spouse has full notice of it. If he or she fails to appear, the entire relief requested may be granted.

Restraining orders may not be used to change parenting functions from one person to another, to distribute property (other than the necessities of life), to set child support, or to create or enforce a right to visitation. They *may*, however, be sought in the same motion as these other items of relief.

The more common acts that restraining orders may be used to protect against are found in Sample 5 (Form DR 04.0150) and Sample 6 (Form DR 04.0170).

These acts, and others like them, may be prevented by an order issued without notice to the opposing spouse. The order must then be served upon him or her. (Often, this is done at the very start of proceedings, and the order is served along with the Summons and Petition for Dissolution.)

Many judges are unwilling to restrict access to the children or family home without notice to the opposing party. This relief should be sought only where the danger of physical harm is readily apparent.

After the order has been served it is enforceable by the police. By law, violation of a court order may be punished by the court with a short jail term and/or a fine, if the restraining order provisions are followed by the following notice in capital letters:

NOTICE: VIOLATION OF THE ABOVE PROVISIONS OF THIS ORDER WITH ACTUAL NOTICE OF THEIR TERMS IS A CRIMINAL OFFENSE UNDER CHAPTER 26.09 R.C.W., AND WILL SUBJECT THE VIOLATOR TO ARREST. RCW 26.09.060(5).

If you have a restraining order, it should be taken to the county sheriff to be recorded on the computer. The sheriff does this without fee. *It is necessary to do this or the police may not enforce your order.* The order must be accompanied by the Law Enforcement Information form (see Sample 7).

i. OTHER TEMPORARY ORDERS

Frequently, other orders are obtained that are maintained until the final order (decree) of dissolution. You may ask for anything that seems necessary. Typical temporary orders deal with residential arrangements for the children, visitation and support, use of the family home or car, etc. See Sample 22 in chapter 4 for the form that these orders would take.

If you are requesting child support, maintenance, or any other financial relief, you must file the financial declaration, shown as Sample 23 in chapter 4.

j. TAX ASPECTS OF SEPARATION AND DIVORCE

If you make payments for the support of your spouse, they may be deducted from your gross income to compute your taxable income, provided that the following conditions are met:

(a) The payments must be made directly to your spouse or to a third party with your spouse's consent and for his or her benefit (e.g., to the mortgage company).

(b) The payments must be for the benefit of the spouse personally — not labeled as "child support."

(c) If the amount of the maintenance exceeds $10,000.00 per year ($833.33 per month), it must continue for a minimum of three years to be a deduction.

(d) The payments must be made according to a written separation agreement or an order of the court.

For tax purposes, your spouse will have to include in his or her income all payments that you properly deduct. If the payments do not meet all of the above conditions, however, they are not deductible and, therefore, your spouse need pay no tax on them.

The most important thing you should remember about the tax consequences of separation agreements, and even court orders calling for payments of money from one spouse or ex-spouse to the other, is that certain kinds of payments are *taxable income* to the recipient, and others are not.

Since all parents, whether married or divorced, are required by law to contribute to the support of their children, there is no tax deduction or credit for such payments.

But separate maintenance (formerly known as alimony) is different. Payments made according to a written separation agreement or court decree that labels them as maintenance are deductible from the gross income of the spouse making the payments and are taxable for the recipient spouse.

Hence, it is in the best interests of the spouse *making* the payments to have them called separate maintenance so they will be a tax savings; likewise, it is in the best interests of the spouse *receiving* the payments to have them labeled child support, so they will not be taxable income.

A compromise can be reached by dividing the total payment into two *specified* amounts, one under each category.

These are just some considerations to take into account in phrasing a separation agreement or, for that matter, in deciding how a court order or Decree of Dissolution should best be worded. The considerations can become quite complicated, and there are certain situations in which you would be best advised to seek the counsel of a lawyer.

The point to be stressed is that a separation agreement can clear up a number of tax difficulties before they arise, and can create a savings for both parties if done correctly.

Currently, the law gives the dependency exemption for the children to the person who has the children in his or her care for the greater part of each year without regard to the amount of financial support given by the other. The physical custodian may give up the exemption by signing a form to be attached to the tax return of the non-custodian that says the custodian is not claiming the exemption. This form can be obtained from your nearest Internal Revenue Service office.

If your decree provides for maintenance or if you are selling real estate as part of your agreement to dissolve your marriage, talk to an attorney or an accountant about the tax consequences of these decisions. Also, if one of you will have a lien against the family home as part of the agreement, talk to a lawyer about the form of the lien as a protection against bankruptcy of the spouse who retains the real estate.

If the family home is to be sold as part of the agreement, consult an accountant regarding the tax impact of that decision. Depending on the timing of the sale, you may save substantial money.

Tax laws change frequently. Be sure to check with a tax adviser before concluding your divorce agreement if any of the problems discussed above pertain to you.

SAMPLE 1
SEPARATION AGREEMENT

SUPERIOR COURT OF WASHINGTON
COUNTY OF   KING

In Re the Marriage of:

JANE HOOD

Wife

and

JOHN HOOD

Husband

NO: _0564_____

SEPARATION AND PROPERTY
SETTLEMENT AGREEMENT

THIS AGREEMENT, made and entered into this 20th day of February, 200–, by and between Jane Hood hereinafter called "wife," and John Hood hereinafter called "husband."

WITNESSETH:

The parties are husband and wife and have been so since the 23rd day of October, 1990 when married at Portland Oregon. The following is a list of all children born to this marriage: Jennifer Lee Hood, born March 25, 1993; Edward John Hood, born October 22, 1997. No additional children are presently contemplated and the wife is not pregnant at this time.

In consequence of disputes and irreconcilable differences, the parties separated on December 18, 200– and from that day forth have been living apart. In view of their intention to continue to live apart for the foreseeable future, they desire to settle their respective property rights and agree on provisions for division of their properties and liabilities and for support of the minor children, along with custody and visitation of those children.

NOW, THEREFORE, in consideration of the mutual promises and agreements contained in this instrument, the parties agree as follows:

1. **Separation:** The parties shall at all times after the date of December 18, 200-, continue to live separate and apart, free from interference from each other, and each party may reside at the place or places he or she may select.

2. **Parenting Plan.**

The agreed Parenting Plan WPF DR 01.0400 is attached. (**Note:** See Sample 15 for an example of a Parenting Plan.)

3. **Child Support**

Paying parent: _____John Hood_____
                                    (name)

Amount(s) per month $ _701.00_ per month per child Date(s) due _on the 15th day_
  _of each month beginning on March 15, 200–_____

Child support shall terminate on: _____

Paid to: _____Jane Hood_____
(Parent directly/Washington State Support Registry)

_____Father_____shall pay_____60____percent of uninsured health care for the children;
(Mother/Father)

other parent shall pay the remainder.

The current total monthly day care expenses of the child(ren) are: _____$100.00_____.

_____Mother_____shall pay __40__percent of day care; other parent shall pay the remainder.
(Mother/Father)

Other costs or special needs: _____

Names of children: _Jennifer Lee Hood and Edward John Hood_____

_____

Both parents shall notify the Washington State Support Registry of any changes of address or employment, if child support is being paid through the Registry.

Both parents are ordered to maintain any health insurance on the minor child(ren) which is available through a present or future employer or other organization, provided that the employer or other organization pays part or all of the premium.

If a support payment as provided for is past due in an amount equal to or greater than the support payable for one month, a notice requiring mandatory payroll deduction may be issued, or other income withholding action under Chapter 26.18 RCW or Chapter RCW 74.20A may be taken, without further notice to the parent obligated to pay support.

The receiving parent may be required to submit an accounting of how the support is being spent to benefit the child(ren).

4. **Income Tax Exemption:** Husband shall be allowed to claim Jennifer Lee Hood as an exemption on his annual income tax return and for the purpose of any applicable tax credits, so long as he is making child support payments under the terms of this Agreement. Wife shall be allowed to claim Edward John Hood as an exemption on her annual income tax return and for the purposes of any applicable tax credits. Each parent will execute all documents necessary to carry out this provision.

5. **Division of Personal Property:** Husband and wife mutually agree that all of the following property will be the sole property of the husband, upon which the wife shall have no claim whatsoever from the date of this agreement:

Furniture now located in the den of the residence which wife and the children are continuing to reside in, together with a 1998 Ford and all household goods, personal effects and other personal property now in the possession or custody or under the control of husband.

Husband and wife mutually agree that all of the following property will be the sole property of the wife, upon which the husband shall have no claim whatsoever from the date of this agreement:

All household goods, furniture, personal effects, and other property now located at the residence in which she is residing with the exception of the furniture in the den, together with a 1996 Dodge Colt station wagon.

6. **Division of Real Property:** For valuable consideration, husband conveys and quit claims all interest that he may have in the residence of the parties commonly known as 1313 Blueview Terrace, Edmonds, Washington, 98020, or more particularly described as:

Lot 1, Block 2, Section 3, Edmonds, Washington

(YOU MUST GIVE LEGAL DESCRIPTION OF REAL ESTATE HERE)

Husband further assigns to wife any and all amounts in the reserve account held by the mortgagee, <u>Washington Federal Savings and Loan Association,</u> for purposes of payment of taxes and insurance on the property described above.

7. **Payment of Debts and other Obligations:** Husband hereby agrees to continue to pay, and hold the wife harmless from any liability thereon, the following described debts and obligations:

Creditor	Approximate Balance
Al's Auto Sales	$1,135.72
Seattle-First National Bank MasterCard	672.56
Household Finance Company	3,073.77
Sears & Roebuck	300.00
Penney's	158.73
Coast Guard Federal Credit Union at Alameda, California	4,400.00
Credit Thrift	934.90
Avco Finance Company	963.75

Wife hereby agrees to continue to pay, and hold the husband harmless from any liability thereon, the following obligations:

Creditor	Approximate Balance
Washington Federal Savings & Loan Association	$31,784.08

This obligation is secured by a Deed of Trust on the residence and real property which is conveyed to wife pursuant to the terms of Paragraph 6 above.

Union 76 Oil Company	Revolving

8. **Payment of Obligations After Date of Execution of this Agreement:** The parties hereto agree that all obligations incurred by husband or wife after the date of the execution of this agreement shall be his or her separation obligation, and he or she will pay in full, when due, all such obligations and shall hold the other party harmless in event of any liability resulting therefrom.

9. **Insurance Policies:** Husband and wife mutually agree that any and all interest and incidents of ownership of any policies of life insurance shall be awarded to the party whose life is insured and that party shall be responsible for making all premium payments thereon. Husband agrees to keep full force and effect his <u>Serviceman's Group Life Insurance policy</u> in the face amount of <u>$20,000.00</u> and to name <u>his children by Jane Hood named on page one above</u> as beneficiaries so long as each is under 18 years of age or is otherwise not emancipated as that term is defined in Paragraph 3. In the event of husband's separation or retirement from <u>active duty with the U.S. Coast Guard</u> or if for any other reason said Serviceman's Group Life Insurance is no longer available to husband or in force the husband agrees to obtain substitute life insurance coverage in a minimum face amount of <u>$20,000.00</u> and to name his children identified above as beneficiaries for a like term.

10. **200– Income Tax Refund:** The parties hereto agree that any tax refund resulting from payment of 200– Federal Income Taxes shall be divided equally between husband and wife.

11. **Income Tax Returns:** It is understood and agreed that husband and wife may file a joint income tax return for any year for which the law authorizes it and which may be affected by this agreement; and each party fully agrees to cooperate in the preparation and execution of any such joint income tax returns.

12. **Pensions, Retirement Pay, Etc.:** Each of the parties has or may acquire in the future, through membership in labor unions, trade associations, fraternal organizations or other organizations of similar type or through his or her employment, life insurance, accident insurance or health insurance on his or her life, and has or may acquire investments in retirement plans, disability insurance plans, and pension or social security rights. The parties agree that any said insurance or rights shall be the sole property of the party through whose membership or employment the same has been or will be acquired.

13. **Representations:** The parties represent to each other:

A. Each has made a full disclosure to the other of his or her current financial condition;

B. Each party understands and agrees that this agreement constitutes the entire contract of the parties. It supersedes all prior understandings or agreements between the parties upon the subject matters covered in this agreement.

C. The parties agree that this Separation and Property Settlement Agreement is fair and equitable at the time of its execution.

14. **Dissolution of Marriage:** The parties hereto acknowledge that wife has filed an action in the Superior Court of King county under Cause No. D564 for the dissolution of the marriage of the parties, and each of the parties to this agreement agrees that he or she will make no prayer for any division of property, support or maintenance inconsistent with any of the terms of this agreement, and the other party shall not contest any terms of said dissolution of marriage which is consistent with this agreement.

Jane Hood
JANE HOOD

John Hood
JOHN HOOD

STATE OF WASHINGTON)
)ss.
COUNTY OF KING)

On this day personally appeared before me Jane Hood to me known to be the individual described in and who executed the foregoing Separation and Property Settlement Agreement, and acknowledged that she signed the same as her free and voluntary act and deed, for the uses and purposes therein mentioned.

GIVEN under my hand and official seal this__20th__day of __Febuary, 200–__ .

I.M. Witness
Notary Public in and for the State of Washington, residing at Edmonds

STATE OF WASHINGTON)
)ss.
COUNTY OF KING)

On this day personally appeared before me John Hood to me known to be the individual described in and who executed the foregoing Separation and Property Settlement Agreement, and acknowledged that he signed the same as his free and voluntary act and deed, for the uses and purposes therein mentioned.

GIVEN under my hand and official seal this__20th__day of __Febuary, 200–__ .

I.C. Ewe
Notary Public in and for the State of Washington, residing at Edmonds

TABLE 1
WASHINGTON STATE CHILD SUPPORT TABLE
MONTHLY BASIC SUPPORT OBLIGATION PER CHILD

(KEY: A = AGE 0-11 B = AGE 12-18)

For income less than $600, the obligation is based upon the resources and living expenses of each household. Minimum support shall not be less than $25 per child per month except when allowed by RCW 26.19.065(2).

Combined Monthly Net Income	One Child Family A	One Child Family B	Two Children Family A	Two Children Family B	Three Children Family A	Three Children Family B	Four Children Family A	Four Children Family B	Five Children Family A	Five Children Family B
600	133	164	103	127	86	106	73	90	63	78
700	155	191	120	148	100	124	85	105	74	91
800	177	218	137	170	115	142	97	120	84	104
900	199	246	154	191	129	159	109	135	95	118
1000	220	272	171	211	143	177	121	149	105	130
1100	242	299	188	232	157	194	133	164	116	143
1200	264	326	205	253	171	211	144	179	126	156
1300	285	352	221	274	185	228	156	193	136	168
1400	307	379	238	294	199	246	168	208	147	181
1500	327	404	254	313	212	262	179	221	156	193
1600	347	428	269	333	225	278	190	235	166	205
1700	367	453	285	352	238	294	201	248	175	217
1800	387	478	300	371	251	310	212	262	185	228
1900	407	503	316	390	264	326	223	275	194	240
2000	427	527	331	409	277	342	234	289	204	252
2100	447	552	347	429	289	358	245	303	213	264
2200	467	577	362	448	302	374	256	316	223	276
2300	487	601	378	467	315	390	267	330	233	288
2400	506	626	393	486	328	406	278	343	242	299
2500	526	650	408	505	341	421	288	356	251	311
2600	534	661	416	513	346	428	293	362	256	316
2700	542	670	421	520	351	435	298	368	259	321
2800	549	679	427	527	356	440	301	372	262	324
2900	556	686	431	533	360	445	305	376	266	328
3000	561	693	436	538	364	449	308	380	268	331
3100	566	699	439	543	367	453	310	383	270	334
3200	569	704	442	546	369	457	312	386	272	336
3300	573	708	445	549	371	459	314	388	273	339
3400	574	710	446	551	372	460	315	389	274	340
3500	575	711	447	552	373	461	316	390	275	341
3600	577	712	448	553	374	462	317	391	276	342
3700	578	713	449	554	375	463	318	392	277	343
3800	581	719	452	558	377	466	319	394	278	344
3900	596	736	463	572	386	477	326	404	284	352
4000	609	753	473	584	395	488	334	413	291	360

TABLE 1—Continued

(KEY: A = AGE 0-11 B = AGE 12-18)

For income less than $600, the obligation is based upon the resources and living expenses of each household. Minimum support shall not be less than $25 per child per month except when allowed by RCW 26.19.065(2).

Combined Monthly Net Income	One Child Family		Two Children Family		Three Children Family		Four Children Family		Five Children Family	
	A	B	A	B	A	B	A	B	A	B
4100	623	770	484	598	404	500	341	422	298	368
4200	638	788	495	611	413	511	350	431	305	377
4300	651	805	506	625	422	522	357	441	311	385
4400	664	821	516	637	431	532	364	449	317	392
4500	677	836	525	649	438	542	371	458	323	400
4600	689	851	535	661	446	552	377	467	329	407
4700	701	866	545	673	455	562	384	475	335	414
4800	713	882	554	685	463	572	391	483	341	422
4900	726	897	564	697	470	581	398	491	347	429
5000	738	912	574	708	479	592	404	500	353	437
5100	751	928	584	720	487	602	411	509	359	443
5200	763	943	593	732	494	611	418	517	365	451
5300	776	959	602	744	503	621	425	525	371	458
5400	788	974	612	756	511	632	432	533	377	466
5500	800	989	622	768	518	641	439	542	383	473
5600	812	1004	632	779	527	651	446	551	389	480
5700	825	1019	641	791	535	661	452	559	395	488
5800	837	1035	650	803	543	671	459	567	401	495
5900	850	1050	660	815	551	681	466	575	407	502
6000	862	1065	670	827	559	691	473	584	413	509
6100	875	1081	680	839	567	701	479	593	418	517
6200	887	1096	689	851	575	710	486	601	424	524
6300	899	1112	699	863	583	721	493	609	430	532
6400	911	1127	709	875	591	731	500	617	436	539
6500	924	1142	718	887	599	740	506	626	442	546
6600	936	1157	728	899	607	750	513	635	448	554
6700	949	1172	737	911	615	761	520	643	454	561
6800	961	1188	747	923	623	770	527	651	460	568
6900	974	1203	757	935	631	780	533	659	466	575
7000	986	1218	767	946	639	790	540	668	472	583

In general setting support under this paragraph does not constitute a deviation. The economic table is presumptive for combined monthly net incomes up to and including five thousand dollars. When combined monthly net income exceeds five thousand dollars, support shall not be set at an amount lower than the presumptive amount of support set for combined monthly net income of five thousand dollars unless the court finds a reason to deviate below that amount. The economic table is advisory but not presumptive for combined monthly net income that exceeds five thousand dollars. When combined monthly net income exceeds seven thousand dollars, the court may set support at an advisory amount of support set for combined monthly net incomes between five thousand and seven thousand dollars or the court may exceed the advisory amount of support set for combined monthly net incomes of seven thousand dollars upon written findings of fact.

Washington State Child Support Schedule

Worksheets (CSW)

Mother_____ Father_____

County_____ Superior Court Case Number_____

Children and Ages:					
Part I: Basic Child Support Obligation					
1. Gross Monthly Income		**Father**		**Mother**	
a. Wages and Salaries		$		$	
b. Interest and Dividend Income		$		$	
c. Business Income		$		$	
d. Spousal Maintenance Received		$		$	
e. Other Income		$		$	
f. Total Gross Monthly Income (add lines 1a through 1e)		$		$	
2. Monthly Deductions from Gross Income					
a. Income Taxes (Federal and State)		$		$	
b. FICA (Soc.Sec.+Medicare)/Self-Employment Taxes		$		$	
c. State Industrial Insurance Deductions		$		$	
d. Mandatory Union/Professional Dues		$		$	
e. Pension Plan Payments		$		$	
f. Spousal Maintenance Paid		$		$	
g. Normal Business Expenses		$		$	
h. Total Deductions from Gross Income (add lines 2a through 2g)		$		$	
3. Monthly Net Income (line 1f minus 2h)		$		$	

4. Combined Monthly Net Income
   (add father's and mother's monthly net incomes from line 3)
   (If combined monthly net income is less than $600, skip to line 7.)
			$		

5. Basic Child Support Obligation (enter total amount in box --------→)
 	
   Child #1_____ Child #3_____
   Child #2_____ Child #4_____
			$		

SAMPLE 2—Continued

	Father	Mother
6. Proportional Share of Income (each parent's net income from line 3 divided by line 4)		
7. Each Parent's Basic Child Support Obligation (multiply each number on line 6 by line 5) (If combined net monthly income on line 4 is less than $600, enter each parent's support obligation of $25 per child. Number of children: _____. Skip to line 15a and enter this amount.)	$	$
Part II: Health Care, Day Care, and Special Child Rearing Expenses		
8. Health Care Expenses		
a. Monthly Health Insurance Premiums Paid for Child(ren)	$	$
b. Uninsured Monthly Health Care Expenses Paid for Child(ren)	$	$
c. Total Monthly Health Care Expenses (line 8a plus line 8b)	$	$
d. Combined Monthly Health Care Expenses (add father's and mother's totals from line 8c)	$	
e. Maximum Ordinary Monthly Health Care (multiply line 5 times .05)	$	
f. Extraordinary Monthly Health Care Expenses (line 8d minus line 8e., if "0" or negative, enter "0")	$	
9. Day Care and Special Child Rearing Expenses		
a. Day Care Expenses	$	$
b. Education Expenses	$	$
c. Long Distance Transportation Expenses	$	$
d. Other Special Expenses (describe)	$	$
	$	$
	$	$
e. Total Day Care and Special Expenses (Add lines 9a through 9d)	$	$
10. Combined Monthly Total Day Care and Special Expenses (add father's and mother's day care and special expenses from line 9e)	$	
11. Total Extraordinary Health Care, Day Care, and Special Expenses (line 8f plus line 10)	$	
12. Each Parent's Obligation for Extraordinary Health Care, Day Care, and Special Expenses (multiply each number on line 6 by line 11)	$	$
Part III: Gross Child Support Obligation		
13. Gross Child Support Obligation (line 7 plus line 12)	$	$
Part IV: Child Support Credits		
14. Child Support Credits		
a. Monthly Health Care Expenses Credit	$	$

SAMPLE 2—Continued

	Father	Mother
b. Day Care and Special Expenses Credit	$	$
c. Other Ordinary Expenses Credit (describe)		
	$	$
d. Total Support Credits (add lines 14a through 14c)	$	$

Part V: Standard Calculation/Presumptive Transfer Payment

15. Standard Calculation	Father	Mother
a. Amount from line 7 if line 4 is below $600. Skip to Part VI.	$	$
b. Line 13 minus line 14d, if line 4 is over $600 (see below if appl.)	$	$
Limitation standards adjustments		
c. Amount on line 15b adjusted to meet 45% net income limitation	$	$
d. Amount on line 15b adjusted to meet need standard limitation	$	$
e. Enter the lowest amount of lines 15b, 15c or 15d:	$	$

Part VI: Additional Factors for Consideration

16. Household Assets (List the estimated present value of all major household assets.)	Father's Household	Mother's Household
a. Real Estate	$	$
b. Stocks and Bonds	$	$
c. Vehicles	$	$
d. Boats	$	$
e. Pensions/IRAs/Bank Accounts	$	$
f. Cash	$	$
g. Insurance Plans	$	$
h. Other (describe)	$	$
	$	$
	$	$

17. Household Debt (List liens against household assets, extraordinary debt.)		
	$	$
	$	$
	$	$
	$	$
	$	$

18. Other Household Income		
a. Income Of Current Spouse (if not the other parent of this action) Name _____	$	$
Name _____	$	$

	Father's Household	Mother's Household
b. Income Of Other Adults In Household Name _____ Name	$ $	$ $
c. Income Of Children (if considered extraordinary) Name _____ Name	$ $	$ $
d. Income From Child Support Name _____ Name	$ $	$ $

Other Household Income (continued)	Father's Household	Mother's Household
e. Income From Assistance Programs Program _____ Program	$ $	$ $
f. Other Income (describe) _____ _____	$ $	$ $
19. Non-Recurring Income (describe) _____ _____	$ $	$ $
20. Child Support Paid For Other Children		
Name/age: _____	$	$
Name/age: _____	$	$
Name/age: _____	$	$

SAMPLE 2—Continued

21. Other Children Living In Each Household (First names and ages)		

22. Other Factors For Consideration

(blank lines for writing)

Signature and Dates

I declare, under penalty of perjury under the laws of the State of Washington, the information contained in these Worksheets is complete, true, and correct.

_____	_____
Mother's Signature	Father's Signature

_____	_____	_____	_____
Date	City	Date	City

_____   _____
Judge/Reviewing Officer   Date

This worksheet has been certified by the State of Washington Office of the Administrator for the Courts. Photocopying of the worksheet is permitted.

SELF-COUNSEL PRESS – DIV WA (20-5) 01

WASHINGTON STATE CHILD SUPPORT SCHEDULE
DEFINITIONS AND STANDARDS

DEFINITIONS

Unless the context clearly requires otherwise, these definitions apply to the standards following this section.

Basic child support obligation: means the monthly child support obligation determined from the economic table based on the parties' combined monthly net income and the number of children for whom support is owed.

Child support schedule: means the standards, economic table, worksheets and instructions, as defined in chapter 26.19 RCW.

Court: means a superior court judge, court commissioner and presiding and reviewing officers who administratively determine or enforce child support orders.

Deviation: means a child support amount that differs from the standard calculation.

Economic table: means the child support table for the basic support obligation provided in RCW 26.19.020.

Instructions: means the instructions developed by the Office of the Administrator for the Courts pursuant to RCW 26.19.050 for use in completing the worksheets.

Standards: means the standards for determination of child support as provided in chapter 26.19 RCW.

Standard calculation: means the presumptive amount of child support owed as determined from the child support schedule before the court considers any reasons for deviation.

Support transfer payment: means the amount of money the court orders one parent to pay to another parent or custodian for child support after determination of the standard calculation and deviations. If certain expenses or credits are expected to fluctuate and the order states a formula or percentage to determine the additional amount or credit on an ongoing basis, the term "support transfer payment" does not mean the additional amount or credit.

Worksheets: means the forms developed by the Office of the Administrator for the Courts pursuant to RCW 26.19.050 for use in determining the amount of child support.

APPLICATION STANDARDS

1. Application of the support schedule: The child support schedule shall be applied:
    a. in each county of the state;
    b. in judicial and administrative proceedings under titles 13, 26 and 74 RCW;
    c. in all proceedings in which child support is determined or modified;
    d. in setting temporary and permanent support;
    e. in automatic modification provisions or decrees entered pursuant to RCW 26.09.100; and
    f. in addition to proceedings in which child support is

determined for minors, to adult children who are dependent on their parents and for whom support is ordered pursuant to RCW 26.09.100.

The provisions of RCW 26.19 for determining child support and reasons for deviation from the standard calculation shall be applied in the same manner by the court, presiding officers and reviewing officers.

2. Written findings of fact supported by the evidence: An order for child support shall be supported by written findings of fact upon which the support determination is based and shall include reasons for any deviation from the standard calculation and reasons for denial of a party's request for deviation from the standard calculation. RCW 26.19.035(2)

3. Completion of worksheets: Worksheets in the form developed by the Office of the Administrator for the Courts shall be completed under penalty of perjury and filed in every proceeding in which child support is determined. The court shall not accept incomplete worksheets or worksheets that vary from the worksheets developed by the Office of the Administrator for the Courts.

4. Court review of the worksheets and order: The court shall review the worksheets and the order setting child support for the adequacy of the reasons set forth for any deviation or denial of any request for deviation and for the adequacy of the amount of support ordered. Each order shall state the amount of child support calculated using the standard calculation and the amount of child support actually ordered. Worksheets shall be attached to the decree or order or if filed separately shall be initialed or signed by the judge and filed with the order.

INCOME STANDARDS

1. Consideration of all income: All income and resources of each parent's household shall be disclosed and considered by the court when the court determines the child support obligation of each parent. Only the income of the parents of the children whose support is at issue shall be calculated for purposes of calculating the basic support obligation. Income and resources of any other person shall not be included in calculating the basic support obligation.

2. Verification of income: Tax returns for the preceding two years and current paystubs shall be provided to verify income and deductions. Other sufficient verification shall be required for income and deductions which do not appear on tax returns or paystubs.

3. Income sources included in gross monthly income: Monthly gross income shall include income from any source, including: salaries; wages; commissions; deferred compensation; overtime; contract-related benefits; income from second jobs; dividends; interest; trust income; severance pay; annuities; capital gains; pension retirement benefits; workers' compensation; unemployment benefits; spousal maintenance actually received; bonuses; social security benefits and disability insurance benefits.

<u>Veterans' disability pensions</u>: Veterans' disability pensions or regular compensation for disability incurred in or aggravated by service in the United States armed forces paid by the Veterans' Administration shall be disclosed to the court. The court may consider either type of compensation as disposable income for purposes of calculating the child support obligation.

4. <u>Income sources excluded from gross monthly income</u>: The following income and resources shall be disclosed but shall not be included in gross income: income of a new spouse or income of other adults in the household; child support received from other relationships; gifts and prizes; temporary assistance for needy families; Supplemental Security Income; general assistance and food stamps. Receipt of income and resources from temporary assistance for needy families, Supplemental Security Income, general assistance and food stamps shall not be a reason to deviate from the standard calculation.

<u>VA aid and attendant care</u>: Aid and attendant care payments to prevent hospitalization paid by the Veterans Administration solely to provide physical home care for a disabled veteran, and special compensation paid under 38 U.S.C. Sec. 314(k) through (r) to provide either special care or special aids, or both to assist with routine daily functions shall be disclosed. The court may not include either aid or attendant care or special medical compensation payments in gross income for purposes of calculating the child support obligation or for purposes of deviating from the standard calculation.

<u>Other aid and attendant care</u>: Payments from any source, other than veterans' aid and attendance allowance or special medical compensation paid under 38 U.S.C. Sec. 314(k) through (r) for services provided by an attendant in case of a disability when the disability necessitates the hiring of the services or an attendant shall be disclosed but shall not be included in gross income and shall not be a reason to deviate from the standard calculation.

5. <u>Determination of net income</u>: The following expenses shall be disclosed and deducted from gross monthly income to calculate net monthly income: federal and state income taxes (see the following paragraph); federal insurance contributions act deductions (FICA); mandatory pension plan payments; mandatory union or professional dues; state industrial insurance premiums; court-ordered spousal maintenance to the extent actually paid; up to two thousand dollars per year in voluntary pension payments actually made if the contributions were made for the two tax years preceding the earlier of the tax year in which the parties separated with intent to live separate and apart or the tax year in which the parties filed for dissolution; and normal business expenses and self-employment taxes for self-employed persons. Justification shall be required for any business expense deduction about which there is a disagreement. Items deducted from gross income shall not be a reason to deviate from the standard calculation.

<u>Allocation of tax exemptions</u>: The parties may agree which parent is entitled to claim the child or children as dependents for federal income tax exemptions. The court may award the exemption or exemptions and order a party to sign the federal income tax dependency exemption waiver. The court may divide the exemptions between the parties, alternate the exemptions between the parties or both.

6. <u>Imputation of income</u>: The court shall impute income to a parent when the parent is voluntarily unemployed or voluntarily underemployed. The court shall determine whether the parent is voluntarily underemployed or voluntarily unemployed based upon that parent's work history, education, health and age or any other relevant factors. A court shall not impute income to a parent who is gainfully employed on a full-time basis, unless the court finds that the parent is voluntarily underemployed and finds that the parent is purposely underemployed to reduce the parent's child support obligation. Income shall not be imputed for an unemployable parent. Income shall not be imputed to a parent to the extent the parent is unemployed or significantly underemployed due to the parent's efforts to comply with court-ordered reunification efforts under chapter 13.34 RCW or under a voluntary placement agreement with an agency supervising the child. In the absence of information to the contrary, a parent's imputed income shall be based on the median income of year-round full-time workers as derived from the United States Bureau of Census, current population reports, or such replacement report as published by the Bureau of Census. (See "Approximate Median Net Monthly Income" chart on page 5.)

ALLOCATION STANDARDS

1. <u>Basic child support</u>: The basic child support obligation derived from the economic table shall be allocated between the parents based on each parent's share of the combined monthly net income.

2. <u>Health care expenses</u>: Ordinary health care expenses are included in the economic table. Monthly health care expenses that exceed 5 percent of the basic support obligation shall be considered extraordinary health care expenses. Extraordinary health care expenses shall be shared by the parents in the same proportion as the basic support obligation.

3. <u>Day care and special child rearing expenses</u>: Day care and special child rearing expenses, such as tuition and long distance transportation costs to and from the parents for visitation purposes, are not included in the economic table. These expenses shall be shared by the parents in the same proportion as the basic child support obligation. RCW 26.19.080

4. The court may exercise its discretion to determine the necessity for and the reasonableness of all amounts ordered in excess of the basic child support obligation.

LIMITATIONS STANDARDS

1. <u>Limit at 45 percent of a parent's net income</u>:
Neither parent's total child support obligation may exceed 45 percent of net income except for good cause shown. Good cause includes but is not limited to possession of substantial wealth, children with day care expenses, special medical need, educational need, psychological need and larger families.

2. <u>Income below six hundred dollars</u>: When combined monthly net income is less than six hundred dollars, a support order of not less than twenty-five dollars per child per month shall be entered for each parent unless the obligor parent establishes that it would be unjust or inappropriate to do so in that particular case. The decision whether there is a sufficient basis to go below the

SAMPLE 3—Continued

presumptive minimum payment must take into consideration the best interests of the child and circumstances of each parent. Such circumstances can include comparative hardship to the affected households, assets or liabilities, and earning capacity.

Basic subsistence limitation: A parent's support obligation shall not reduce his or her net income below the need standard for one person established pursuant to RCW 74.04.770, except for the presumptive minimum payment of twenty-five dollars per child per month or in cases where the court finds reasons for deviation. This section shall not be construed to require monthly substantiation of income. (See www.nwjustice.org for the "Washington State Need Standard Chart.")

3.   Income above five thousand and seven thousand dollars: In general setting support under this paragraph does not constitute a deviation. The economic table is presumptive for combined monthly net incomes up to and including five thousand dollars. When combined monthly net income exceeds five thousand dollars, support shall not be set at an amount lower than the presumptive amount of support set for combined monthly net incomes of five thousand dollars unless the court finds a reason to deviate below that amount. The economic table is advisory but not presumptive for combined monthly net income that exceeds five thousand dollars. When combined monthly net income exceeds seven thousand dollars, the court may set support at an advisory amount of support set for combined monthly net incomes between five thousand and seven thousand dollars or the court may exceed the advisory amount of support for combined monthly net income of seven thousand dollars upon written findings of fact.

DEVIATION STANDARDS

1.   Reasons for deviation from the standard calculation include but are not limited to the following:

a.   Sources of income and tax planning: The court may deviate from the standard calculation after consideration of the following:
i.   Income of a new spouse if the parent who is married to the new spouse is asking for a deviation based on any other reason. Income of a new spouse is not, by itself, a sufficient reason for deviation;
ii.   Income of other adults in the household if the parent who is living with the other adult is asking for a deviation based on any other reason. Income of the other adults in the household is not, by itself, a sufficient reason for deviation;
iii.   Child support actually received from other relationships;
iv.   Gifts;
v.   Prizes;
vi.   Possession of wealth, including but not limited to savings, investments, real estate holdings and business interests, vehicles, boats, pensions, bank accounts, insurance plans or other assets;
vii.   Extraordinary income of a child; or
viii.   Tax planning considerations. A deviation for tax planning may be granted only if the child would not receive a lesser economic benefit due to the tax planning.

b.   Nonrecurring income: The court may deviate from the standard calculation based on a finding that a particular source of income included in the calculation of the basic support obligation is not a recurring source of income. Depending on the circumstances, nonrecurring income may include overtime, contract-related benefits, bonuses or income from second jobs. Deviations for nonrecurring income shall be based on a review of the nonrecurring income received in the previous two calendar years.

c.   Debt and high expenses: The court may deviate from the standard calculation after consideration of the following expenses:
i.   Extraordinary debt not voluntarily incurred;
ii.   A significant disparity in the living costs of the parents due to conditions beyond their control;
iii.   Special needs of disabled children; or
iv.   Special medical, educational or psychological needs of the children.
v.   Costs anticipated to be incurred by the parents in compliance with court-ordered reunification efforts under chapter 13.34 RCW or under a voluntary placement agreement with an agency supervising the child.

d.   Residential schedule: The court may deviate from the standard calculation if the child spends a significant amount of time with the parent who is obligated to make a support transfer payment. The court may not deviate on that basis if the deviation will result in insufficient funds in the household receiving the support to meet the basic needs of the child or if the child is receiving temporary assistance for needy families. When determining the amount of the deviation, the court shall consider evidence concerning the increased expenses to a parent making support transfer payments resulting from the significant amount of time spent with that parent and shall consider the decreased expenses, if any, to the party receiving the support resulting from the significant amount of time the child spends with the parent making the support transfer payment.

e.   Children from other relationships: The court may deviate from the standard calculation when either or both of the parents before the court have children from other relationships to whom the parent owes a duty of support.
i.   The child support schedule shall be applied to the mother, father and children of the family before the court to determine the presumptive amount of support.
ii.   Children from other relationships shall not be counted in the number of children for purposes of determining the basic support obligation and the standard calculation.
iii.   When considering a deviation from the standard calculation for children from other relationships, the court may consider only other children to whom the parent owes a duty of support. The court may consider court-ordered payments of child support for children from other relationships only to the extent that the support is actually paid.

WSCSS-Schedule 09-01-2000   **Page 3**

iv. When the court has determined that either or both parents have children from other relationships, deviations under this section shall be based on consideration of the total circumstances of both households. All child support obligations paid, received and owed for all children shall be disclosed and considered.

2. All income and resources of the parties before the court, new spouses, and other adults in the household shall be disclosed and considered as provided. The presumptive amount of support shall be determined according to the child support schedule. Unless specific reasons for deviation are set forth in the written findings of fact and are supported by the evidence, the court shall order each parent to pay the amount of support determined by using the standard calculation.

3. The court shall enter findings that specify reasons for any deviation or any denial of a party's request for any deviation from the standard calculation made by the court. The court shall not consider reasons for deviation until the court determines the standard calculation for each parent.

4. When reasons exist for deviation, the court shall exercise discretion in considering the extent to which the factors would affect the support obligation.

5. Agreement of the parties is not by itself adequate reason for any deviations from the standard calculations.

POST-SECONDARY EDUCATION STANDARDS

1. The child support schedule shall be advisory and not mandatory for post-secondary educational support.

2. When considering whether to order support for post-secondary educational expenses, the court shall determine whether the child is in fact dependent and is relying upon the parents for the reasonable necessities of life. The court shall exercise its discretion when determining whether and for how long to award post-secondary educational support based upon consideration of factors that include but are not limited to the following: age of the child; the child's needs; the expectations of the parties for their children when the parents were together; the child's prospects, desires, aptitudes, abilities or disabilities; the nature of the post-secondary education sought and the parent's level of education, standard of living and current and future resources. Also to be considered are the amount and type of support that the child would have been afforded if the parents had stayed together.

3. The child must enroll in an accredited academic or vocational school, must be actively pursuing a course of study commensurate with the child's vocational goals and must be in good academic standing as defined by the institution. The court-ordered post-secondary educational support shall be automatically suspended during the period or periods the child fails to comply with these conditions.

4. The child shall also make available all academic records and grades to both parents as a condition of receiving post-secondary educational support. Each parent shall have full and equal access to the post-secondary education records as provided by statute (RCW 26.09.225).

5. The court shall not order the payment of post-secondary educational expenses beyond the child's twenty-third birthday, except for exceptional circumstances, such as mental, physical or emotional disabilities.

6. The court shall direct that either or both parents' payments for post-secondary educational expenses are made directly to the educational institution if feasible. If direct payments are not feasible, then the court in its discretion may order that either or both parents' payments are made directly to the child if the child does not reside with either parent. If the child resides with one of the parents, the court may direct that the parent making the support transfer payments make the payments to the child or to the parent who has been receiving the support transfer payments.

WASHINGTON STATE CHILD SUPPORT SCHEDULE
WORKSHEETS INSTRUCTIONS

WASHINGTON STATE CHILD SUPPORT SCHEDULE
INSTRUCTIONS FOR WORKSHEETS

Fill in the names and ages of only those children whose support is at issue.

PART I: BASIC CHILD SUPPORT OBLIGATION

Pursuant to INCOME STANDARD #1: Consideration of all income, "only the income of the parents of the children whose support is at issue shall be calculated for purposes of calculating the basic support obligation."

Pursuant to INCOME STANDARD #2: Verification of income, "tax returns for the preceding two years and current paystubs are required for income verification purposes. Other sufficient verification shall be required for income and deductions which do not appear on tax returns or paystubs."

GROSS MONTHLY INCOME

Gross monthly income is defined under INCOME STANDARD #3: Income sources included in gross monthly income.

Income exclusions are defined under INCOME STANDARD #4: Income sources excluded from gross monthly income. Excluded income must be disclosed and listed in Part VI of the worksheets.

Monthly Average of Income:

- If income varies during the year, divide the annual total of the income by 12.

- If paid weekly, multiply the weekly income by 52 and divide by 12.

- If paid every other week, multiply the two-week income by 26 and divide by 12.

- If paid twice a month (bi-monthly), multiply the bi-monthly income by 24 and divide by 12.

If a parent is unemployed, underemployed or the income of a parent is unknown, refer to "INCOME STANDARD #6: Imputation of income."

In the absence of information to the contrary, a parent's imputed income shall be based on the following table.

Approximate Median Net Monthly Income

MALE	age	FEMALE
$1,363	15-24	$1,222
$2,154	25-34	$1,807
$2,610	35-44	$1,957
$2,846	45-54	$2,051
$2,880	55-64	$1,904
$2,828	65 +	$1,940

U.S. Bureau of the Census, Money Income in the United States: 1998, Current Population Reports, Median Income of People by Selected Characteristics: 1998, Full-Time, Year-Round Workers, Table 7

[Net income has been determined by subtracting FICA (7.65 percent) and the tax liability for a single person (one withholding allowance).]

LINE 1a, Wages and Salaries: Enter the average monthly total of all salaries, wages, contract-related benefits, income from second jobs and bonuses.

LINE 1b, Interest and Dividend Income: Enter the average monthly total of dividends and interest income.

LINE 1c, Business Income: Enter the average monthly income from self-employment.

LINE 1d, Spousal Maintenance Received: Enter the monthly amount of spousal maintenance actually received.

LINE 1e, Other Income: Enter the average monthly total of other income. (Other income includes, but is not limited to: trust income, severance pay, annuities, capital gains, pension retirement benefits, workers compensation, unemployment benefits, social security benefits and disability insurance benefits.)

LINE 1f, Total Gross Monthly Income: Add the monthly income amounts for each parent (lines 1a through 1e) and enter the totals on line 1f.

MONTHLY DEDUCTIONS FROM GROSS INCOME

Allowable monthly deductions from gross income are defined under INCOME STANDARD #5: Determination of net income.

Monthly Average of Deductions: If a deduction is annual or varies during the year, divide the annual total of the deduction by 12 to determine a monthly amount.

LINE 2a, Income Taxes: Enter the monthly amount actually owed for state and federal income taxes. (The amount of income tax withheld on a paycheck may not be the actual amount of income tax owed due to tax refund, etc. It is appropriate to consider tax returns from prior years as indicating the actual amount of income tax owed if income has not changed.)

LINE 2b, FICA/Self Employment Taxes: Enter the total monthly amount of FICA, Social Security, Medicare and Self-employment taxes owed.

LINE 2c, State Industrial Insurance Deductions: Enter the monthly amount of state industrial insurance deductions.

LINE 2d, Mandatory Union/Professional Dues: Enter the monthly cost of mandatory union or professional dues.

SELF-COUNSEL PRESS – DIV WA INSTRUCT (1-4) 01

LINE 2e, <u>Pension Plan Payments</u>: Enter the monthly cost of pension plan payments. (For information regarding limitations on the allowable deduction of voluntary pension plan payments, refer to INCOME STANDARD #5: <u>Determination of net income</u>.)

LINE 2f, <u>Spousal Maintenance Paid</u>: Enter the monthly amount of spousal maintenance actually paid pursuant to a court order.

LINE 2g, <u>Normal Business Expenses</u>: If self-employed, enter the amount of normal business expenses. (Pursuant to INCOME STANDARD #5: <u>Determination of net income</u>, "justification shall be required for any business expense deduction about which there is a disagreement.")

LINE 2h, <u>Total Deductions From Gross Income</u>: Add the monthly deductions for each parent (lines 2a through 2g) and enter the totals on line 2h.

LINE 3, <u>Monthly Net Income</u>: For each parent subtract total deductions (line 2h) from total gross monthly income (line 1f) and enter these amounts on line 3.

LINE 4, <u>Combined Monthly Net Income</u>: Add the parents' monthly net incomes (line 3) and enter the total on line 4.

If the combined income on line 4 is less than $600, skip to line 7.

LINE 5, <u>Basic Child Support Obligation</u>: In the work area provided on line 5, enter the basic support obligation amounts determined for each child. Add these amounts together and enter the total in the box on line 5. (To determine a per child basic support obligation, see the following economic table instructions.)

ECONOMIC TABLE INSTRUCTIONS

(See page 20-21 of the *Divorce Guide for Washington* for Economic Table.)

To use the Economic Table to determine an individual support amount for each child:

- **Locate in the left-hand column the combined monthly net income amount closest to the amount entered on line 4 of Worksheet** (round up when the combined monthly net income falls halfway between the two amounts in the left-hand column);

- **locate on the top row the family size for the number of children for whom child support is being determined** (when determining family size for the required worksheets, do not include children from other relationships); and

- **circle the two numbers in the columns listed below the family size that are across from the net income amount. The amount in the "A" column is the basic support amount for a child up to age 11. The amount in the "B" column is the basic support amount for a child 12 years of age or older.**

LINE 6, <u>Proportional Share of Income</u>: Divide the monthly net income for each parent (line 3) by the combined monthly net income (line 4) and enter these amounts on line 6. (The entries on line 6 when added together should equal 1.00.)

LINE 7, <u>Each Parent's Basic Child Support Obligation</u>: Multiply the total basic child support obligation (amount in box on line 5) by the income share proportion for each parent (line 6) and enter these amounts on line 7. (The amounts entered on line 7 added together should equal the amount entered on line 5.)

If the combined monthly net income on line 4 is less than $600, enter on line 7 each parent's support obligation, which is the presumptive minimum amount of $25 multiplied by the number of children. Then skip to line 15(a) and enter the same amount.

<u>PART II: HEALTH CARE, DAY CARE, AND SPECIAL CHILD REARING EXPENSES</u>

Pursuant to ALLOCATION STANDARD #4: "the court may exercise its discretion to determine the necessity for and the reasonableness of all amounts ordered in excess of the basic child support obligation."

Pursuant to ALLOCATION STANDARD #2: Health care expenses and #3: Day care and special child rearing expenses, extraordinary health care, day care and special child rearing expenses shall be shared by the parents in the same proportion as the basic support obligation. NOTE: The court order should reflect that extraordinary health care, day care and special child rearing expenses not listed should be apportioned by the same percentage as the basic child support obligation.

Monthly Average of Expenses: If a health care, day care, or special child rearing expense is annual or varies during the year, divide the annual total of the expense by 12 to determine a monthly amount.

HEALTH CARE EXPENSES

LINE 8a, <u>Monthly Health Insurance Premiums Paid For Child(ren)</u>: List the monthly amount paid by each parent for health care insurance for the child(ren) of the relationship. (When determining an insurance premium amount, do not include the portion of the premium paid by an employer or other third party and/or the portion of the premium that covers the parent or other household members.)

LINE 8b, <u>Uninsured Monthly Health Care Expenses Paid For Child(ren)</u>: List the monthly amount paid by each parent for the child(ren)'s health care expenses not reimbursed by insurance.

LINE 8c, <u>Total Monthly Health Care Expenses</u>: For each parent add the health insurance premium payments (line 8a) to the uninsured health care payments (line 8b) and enter these amounts on line 8c.

SELF-COUNSEL PRESS – DIV WA INSTRUCT (2-4) 01

LINE 8d, Combined Monthly Health Care Expenses: Add the parents' total health care payments (line 8c) and enter this amount on line 8d.

LINE 8e, Maximum Ordinary Monthly Health Care: Multiply the basic support obligation (line 5) times .05.

LINE 8f, Extraordinary Monthly Health Care Expenses: Subtract the maximum monthly health care deduction (line 8e) from the combined monthly health care payments (line 8d) and enter this amount on line 8f. (If the resulting answer is "0" or a negative number, enter a "0".)

DAY CARE AND SPECIAL CHILD REARING EXPENSES

LINE 9a, Day Care Expenses: Enter average monthly day care costs.

LINE 9b, Education Expenses: Enter the average monthly costs of tuition and other related educational expenses.

LINE 9c, Long Distance Transportation Expenses: Enter the average monthly costs of long distance travel incurred pursuant to the residential or visitation schedule.

LINE 9d, Other Special Expenses: Identify any other special expenses and enter the average monthly cost of each.

LINE 9e, Total Day Care and Special Expenses: Add the monthly expenses for each parent (lines 9a through 9d) and enter these totals on line 9e.

LINE 10, Combined Monthly Total of Day Care and Special Expenses: Add the parents' total expenses (line 9e) and enter this total on line 10.

LINE 11, Total Extraordinary Health Care, Day Care and Special Expenses: Add the extraordinary health care payments (line 8f) to the combined monthly total of day care and special expenses (line 10) and enter this amount on line 11.

LINE 12, Each Parent's Obligation For Extraordinary Health Care, Day Care And Special Expenses: Multiply the total extraordinary health care, day care, and special expense amount (line 11) by the income proportion for each parent (line 6) and enter these amounts on line 12.

PART III: GROSS CHILD SUPPORT OBLIGATION

LINE 13, Gross Child Support Obligation: For each parent add the basic child support obligation (line 7) to the obligation for extraordinary health care, day care and special expenses (line 12). Enter these amounts on line 13.

PART IV: CHILD SUPPORT CREDITS

Child support credits are provided in cases where parents make direct payments to third parties for the cost of goods and services which are included in the standard calculation support obligation (e.g., payments to an insurance company or a day care provider).

LINE 14a, Monthly Health Care Expenses Credit: Enter the total monthly health care expenses amounts from line 8c for each parent.

LINE 14b, Day Care And Special Expenses Credit: Enter the total day care and special expenses amounts from line 9e for each parent.

LINE 14c, Other Ordinary Expense Credit: If approval of an other ordinary expense credit is being requested, in the space provided, specify the expense and enter the average monthly cost in the column of the parent to receive the credit. (It is generally assumed that ordinary expenses are paid in accordance with the child's residence. If payment of a specific ordinary expense does not follow this assumption, the parent paying for this expense may request approval of an ordinary expense credit. This credit is discretionary with the court.)

LINE 14d, Total Support Credits: For each parent, add the entries on lines 14 a through c and enter the totals on line 14d.

PART V: STANDARD CALCULATION/ PRESUMPTIVE TRANSFER PAYMENT

LINE 15a, if combined monthly income on line 4 is below $600, for each parent enter the amount from line 7 on line 15a. If the court does not deviate from the standard calculation, the transfer payment should equal the amount in the paying person's column. Skip to Part VI.

LINE 15b, if combined income on line 4 is $600 or more, for each parent subtract the total support credits (line 14d) from the gross child support obligation (line 13) and enter the resulting amounts on line 15b.

LINE 15c, Multiply line 3 by .45. If that amount is less than 15(b) enter that amount on line 15(c). If the amount is equal to or greater than line 15(b) leave line 15(c) blank. You do not qualify for the 45% net income limitation standard.

LINE 15d, Subtract the standard need amount (page 3, Basic subsistence limitation) from the amount on Line 3 for each parent. If that amount is less than Line 15(b) enter that amount or $25 per child, whichever is greater, on line 15(d). If that amount is equal to or greater than line 15(b) leave line 15(d) blank. You do not qualify for a need standard limitation.

LINE 15e, Enter the lowest amount from lines 15(b), 15(c) and 15(d) on line 15(e). If the court does not deviate from the standard calculation, the transfer payment should equal the amount in the paying person's column.

PART VI: ADDITIONAL FACTORS FOR CONSIDERATION

Pursuant to INCOME STANDARD #1: Consideration of all income, "all income and resources of each parent's household shall be disclosed and considered by the court when the court determines the child support obligation of each parent."

SELF-COUNSEL PRESS – DIV WA INSTRUCT (3-4) 01

LINE 16 a-h, <u>Household Assets</u>: Enter the estimated present value of assets of the household.

LINE 17, <u>Household Debt</u>: Describe and enter the amount of liens against assets owned by the household and/or any extraordinary debt.

OTHER HOUSEHOLD INCOME

LINE 18a, <u>Income of Current Spouse</u>: If a parent is currently married to someone other than the parent of the child(ren) for whom support is being determined, list the name and enter the income of the present spouse.

LINE 18b, <u>Income of Other Adults In The Household</u>: List the names and enter the incomes of other adults residing in the household.

LINE 18c, <u>Income of Children</u>: If the amount is considered to be extraordinary, list the name and enter the income of children residing in the home.

LINE 18d, <u>Income from Child Support</u>: List the name of the child(ren) for whom support is received and enter the amount of the support income.

LINE 18e, <u>Income from Assistance Programs</u>: List the program and enter the amount of any income received from assistance programs. (Assistance programs include, but are not limited to: temporary assistance for needy families, SSI, general assistance, food stamps and aid and attendance allowances.)

LINE 18f, <u>Other Income</u>: Describe and enter the amount of any other income of the household. (Include income from gifts and prizes on this line.)

LINE 19, <u>Nonrecurring Income</u>: Describe and enter the amount of any income included in the calculation of gross income (LINE 1f) which is nonrecurring. (Pursuant to DEVIATION STANDARD #1b: Nonrecurring income," depending on the circumstances, nonrecurring income may include overtime, contract-related benefits, bonuses or income from second jobs.")

LINE 20, <u>Child Support Paid for Other Children</u>: List the names and ages and enter the amount of child support paid for other children.

LINE 21, <u>Other Children Living in Each Household</u>: List the names and ages of children, other than those for whom support is being determined, who are living in each household.

LINE 22, <u>Other Factors For Consideration</u>: In the space provided list any other factors that should be considered in determining the child support obligation. (For information regarding other factors for consideration, refer to DEVIATION STANDARDS.)

Nonparental Custody Cases: When the children do not reside with either parent, the household income and resources of the children's custodian(s) should be listed on line 22.

SELF-COUNSEL PRESS – DIV WA INSTRUCT (4-4) 01

SAMPLE 5
MOTION/DECLARATION FOR EX PARTE RESTRAINING ORDER AND FOR ORDER TO SHOW CAUSE

SUPERIOR COURT OF WASHINGTON
COUNTY OF   SPOKANE

In re the Marriage of:

SUE SNOOPIE

                    Petitioner,

and

SAM SNOOPIE

                    Respondent.

NO. XX-X-XXXXX-X

MOTION/DECLARATION FOR EX PARTE RESTRAINING ORDER AND FOR ORDER TO SHOW CAUSE **(MTAF)**

I. MOTION

Based upon the declaration below, the undersigned moves the court for a temporary order and order to show cause.

1.1   EX PARTE RESTRAINING ORDER.

A temporary restraining order should be granted without written or oral notice to the other party or the other party's lawyer because immediate and irreparable injury, loss, or damage will result before other party or the other party's lawyer can be heard in opposition. This order should restrain or enjoin:

[X]   the [X] husband [ ] wife from transferring, removing, encumbering, concealing or in any way disposing of any property except in the usual course of business or for the necessities of life and requiring each party to notify the other of any extraordinary expenditures made after the order is issued.

[X]   the [X] husband [ ] wife from molesting or disturbing the peace of the other party or of any child.

[ ]   _____ [Name] from going onto the grounds of or entering the [ ] parties' shared residence [ ] residence of _____ [Name]. _____ [Name] waives confidentiality of the address which is _____ [Address].

[X]   the [X] husband [ ] wife from going onto the grounds of or entering the home. work place or school of the other party or the day care or school of these children: _____

_____

[X]   the [X] husband [ ] wife from knowingly coming within or knowingly remaining within _____ (distance) of the home, work place or school of the other party or the day care or school of these children: _____.

[X]   the [X] husband [ ] wife from removing any of the children from the state of Washington.

[X]   the [X] husband [ ] wife from assigning. transferring, borrowing, lapsing, surrendering or changing entitlement of any insurance policies of either or both parties whether medical, health, life or auto insurance.

MTNIDECL FOR EX PARTE RESTRAINING ORD (MTAF) - Page 1 of 4
WPF DR 04.0150 (9/2001) - CR 65 (b); RCW 26.09.060.

SELF-COUNSEL PRESS – DIV WA (25-1) 01

[ ]   other:

The other party should be required to appear and show cause why these restraints should not be continued in full force and effect pending final determination of this action.

1.2   SURRENDER OF DEADLY WEAPONS.

[X]   Does not apply.
[ ]   **(IF THIS BOX IS CHECKED, CLEAR AND CONVINCING REASONS FOR THIS REQUEST MUST BE PRESENTED IN PARAGRAPH 2.3 BELOW.)** The court should require the [ ] husband [ ] wife to surrender any deadly weapon in his or her immediate possession or control or subject to his or her immediate possession or control to the sheriff of the county having jurisdiction of this proceeding, to his or her lawyer or to a person designated by the court.

1.3   OTHER TEMPORARY RELIEF.

[ ]   Does not apply.
[X]   The [X] husband [ ] wife should also be required to appear and show cause why the court should not enter a temporary order which:

        [X]   orders temporary maintenance.
        [X]   orders child support as determined pursuant to the Washington State Child Support Schedule.
        [X]   approves the parenting plan which is proposed by the [ ] husband [ ] wife.
        [ ]   makes each party immediately responsible for their own future debts whether incurred by credit card or loan, security interest or mortgage.
        [ ]   divides responsibility for the debts of the parties.
        [ ]   authorizes the family home to be occupied by the [ ] husband [ ] wife.
        [ ]   orders the use of property.
        [ ]   requires the [ ] husband [ ] wife to vacate the family home.
        [X]   requires the [X] husband [ ] wife to pay temporary attorney's fees, other professional fees and costs in the amount of $ 1,000 to:

                THE PETITIONER IN ORDER TO RETAIN A LAWYER

        [ ]   appoints a guardian ad litem on behalf of the minor children.
        [ ]   other:

1.4   OTHER.

MTN/DECL FOR EX PARTE RESTRAINING ORD (MTAF) - Page 2 of 4
WPF DR 04.0150 (9/2001) - CR 65 (b); RCW 26.09.060.

SELF-COUNSEL PRESS – DIV WA (25-2) 01

Dated: _____JANUARY 5, 200-_____

Sue Snoopie
Signature of Lawyer or Moving Party

SUE SNOOPIE
Print or Type Name

II. DECLARATION

2.1 INJURY TO BE PREVENTED.

The ex parte restraining order requested in paragraph 1.1 above is to prevent the following injury [define the injury]:

THE RESPONDENT HAS ASSAULTED ME IN THE PAST AND I FEAR PHYSICAL INJURY

2.2 REASONS WHY THE INJURY MAY BE IRREPARABLE.

This injury may be irreparable because:

ONE CANNOT BE ADEQUATELY COMPENSATED FOR PHYSICAL INJURY

2.3 CLEAR AND CONVINCING REASONS WHY WEAPONS SHOULD BE SURRENDERED.

[X] Does not apply.
[ ] The [ ] husband [ ] wife should be required to surrender any deadly weapons as requested in paragraph 1.2 above because of following clear and convincing reasons:

MTN/DECL FOR EX PARTE RESTRAINING ORD (MTAF) - Page 3 of 4
WPF DR 04.0150 (9/2001) - CR 65 (b); RCW 26.09.060.

SELF-COUNSEL PRESS – DIV WA (25-3) 01

39

2.4   REASONS FOR A TEMPORARY ORDER.

[ ]   Does not apply.

[X]   It is necessary that the court issue a temporary order with the relief requested in paragraph 1.3
above for the reason set forth below:

I FEAR THAT THE RESPONDENT WILL ASSAULT ME. ALSO, I FEAR
THAT HE WILL BEGIN GIVING AWAY OR SELLING OUR ASSETS.

I declare under penalty of perjury under the laws of the state of Washington that the foregoing is true and correct.

Signed at   SPOKANE, WASHINGTON   , on   JANUARY 5, 200-   .
                  [City and State]   [Date]

Sue Snoopie
Signature

SUE SNOOPIE
Print or Type Name

DO NOT ATTACH FINANCIAL RECORDS TO THIS DECLARATION. FINANCIAL RECORDS SHOULD BE
SERVED ON THE OTHER PARTY AND FILED WITH THE COURT SEPARATELY USING THE SEALED
FINANCIAL SOURCE DOCUMENTS COVER SHEET (WPF DRPSCU 09.0220). IF FILED SEPARATELY
USING THE COVER SHEET, THE RECORDS WILL BE SEALED TO PROTECT YOUR PRIVACY
(ALTHOUGH THEY WILL BE AVAILABLE TO THE OTHER PARTIES IN THE CASE, THEIR
ATTORNEYS, AND CERTAIN OTHER INTERESTED PERSONS. SEE GR 22 (C)(2)).

III. EFFORTS TO GIVE OTHER PARTY NOTICE.

The following efforts have been made to give the other party or other party's lawyer notice and the following
reasons exist why notice should not be required:

I HAVE NOT GIVEN NOTICE BECAUSE I BELIEVE THAT DOING SO WOULD
RESULT IN THE INJURIES I FEAR.

Dated: JANUARY 5, 200-

Sue Snoopie
Signature of Lawyer or Moving Party (if not represented
by a lawyer)

SUE SNOOPIE
Print or Type Name

MTN/DECL FOR EX PARTE RESTRAINING ORD (MTAF) - Page 4 of 4
WPF DR 04.0150 (9/2001) - CR 65 (b); RCW 26.09.060.

SELF-COUNSEL PRESS – DIV WA (25-4) 01

SUPERIOR COURT OF WASHINGTON
COUNTY OF

In re the Marriage of:	**NO.**
Petitioner,	EX PARTE RESTRAINING ORDER/ORDER TO SHOW CAUSE (TPROTSC)
and	
Respondent.	[ ] Clerk's Action Required

Restraining Order Summary:
    [ ] Does not apply.
    [ ] Restraining Order Summary is set forth below:

Name of person(s) restrained: _____, Name of
person(s) protected:_____**See paragraph 4.1.**

> **VIOLATION OF A RESTRAINING ORDER IN PARAGRAPH 4.1 BELOW WITH ACTUAL KNOWLEDGE OF ITS TERMS IS A CRIMINAL OFFENSE UNDER CHAPTER 26.50 RCW AND WILL SUBJECT THE VIOLATOR TO ARREST. RCW 26.09.060.**

I. SHOW CAUSE ORDER.

It is ordered that the [ ] husband [ ] wife appear and show cause, if any, why the restraints below should not be continued in full force and effect pending final determination of this action and why the other relief, if any, requested in paragraph 1.3 of the motion should not be granted. A hearing has been set for the following date, time and place:

Date: _____ Time: _____ a.m./p.m.

Place: _____ Room/Department: _____

FAILURE TO APPEAR MAY RESULT IN A TEMPORARY ORDER BEING ENTERED BY THE COURT THAT GRANTS THE RELIEF REQUESTED IN THE MOTION WITHOUT FURTHER NOTICE.

II. BASIS

A motion for a temporary restraining order without written or oral notice to the [ ] husband [ ] wife or that party's lawyer has been made to this court.

III. FINDINGS

The court adopts paragraphs 2.1, 2.2, and 2.4 of the Motion/Declaration for an Ex Parte Restraining Order and for an Order to Show Cause (Form WPF DR 04.0150) as its findings, except as follows:

IV. ORDER

It is ORDERED that:

4.1   RESTRAINING ORDER.

VIOLATION OF A RESTRAINING ORDER IN PARAGRAPH 4.1 WITH ACTUAL NOTICE OF ITS TERMS IS A CRIMINAL OFFENSE UNDER CHAPTER 26.50 RCW AND WILL SUBJECT THE VIOLATOR TO ARREST. RCW 26.09.060.

[ ]   Does not apply.

[ ]   The [ ] husband [ ] wife is restrained and enjoined from molesting or disturbing the peace of the other party or of any child.

[ ]   The [ ] husband [ ] wife is restrained and enjoined from going onto the grounds of or entering the home, work place or school of the other party or the day care or school of the following named children: _____.

[ ]   The [ ] husband [ ] wife is restrained and enjoined from knowingly coming within or knowingly remaining within _____ (distance) of the home, work place or school of the other party or the day care or school of these children: _____.

[ ]   CLERK'S ACTION. The clerk of the court shall forward a copy of this order, on or before the next judicial day, to _____ [name of the appropriate law enforcement agency] which shall enter this order into any computer-based criminal intelligence system available in this state used by law enforcement agencies to list outstanding warrants. (**A law enforcement information sheet must be completed by the party or the party's attorney and provided with this order before this order will be entered into the law enforcement computer system.**)

4.2   OTHER RESTRAINING ORDERS.

[ ]   The [ ] husband [ ] wife is restrained and enjoined from transferring, removing, encumbering, concealing or in any way disposing of any property except in the usual course of business or for the necessities of life and requiring each party to notify the other of any extraordinary expenditures made after the order is issued.

[ ]   The [ ] husband [ ] wife is restrained and enjoined from removing any of the children from the state of Washington.

[ ]   The [ ] husband [ ] wife is restrained and enjoined from assigning, transferring, borrowing, lapsing, surrendering or changing entitlement of any insurance policies of either or both parties whether medical, health, life or auto insurance.

EX PARTE RESTRAINING ORD (TPROTSC) - Page 2 of 3
WPF DR 04.0170 (9/2001) - CR 65 (b); RCW 26.09.060   SELF-COUNSEL PRESS – DIV WA (26-2) 01

42

SAMPLE 6—Continued

[ ]   Other:

4.3   SURRENDER OF DEADLY WEAPONS.

[ ]   Does not apply.
[ ]   It is ordered that _____ [Name] surrender any deadly weapon in his or her immediate possession or control or subject to his or her immediate possession or control to:

    [ ]   the _____ [Name of county] County sheriff.
    [ ]   _____ [Name].

The court finds that irreparable injury could result if an order is not issued until the time for response has elapsed. (See RCW 26.09.060(2)(b).)

4.4   EXPIRATION DATE.

This order shall expire on the hearing date set forth above or 14 days from the date of issuance, which ever is sooner, unless otherwise extended by the court.

4.5   WAIVER OF BOND.

[ ]   Does not apply.
[ ]   The filing of a bond or the posting of security is waived.

4.6   Other:

Dated: _____ at _____ a.m./p.m.   _____
    JUDGE/COMMISSIONER

Presented by:

_____
Signature

_____
Print or Type Name

DO NOT SERVE OR SHOW THIS SHEET TO THE RESTRAINED PERSON

COURT CLERKS: Give this form to Law Enforcement. DO NOT FILE in the court file.	Case Number XX-X-XXXXX-X

☐ Domestic Violence   ☐ Dissolution/Separation/Invalidity/Nonparental Custody/Paternity   ☐ Antiharassment

LAW ENFORCEMENT INFORMATION

This completed form is required by law enforcement. This information is **necessary** to serve, enforce and enter your order into the state wide law enforcement computer. Fill in the following information as completely as possible. Type or print only.

RESTRAINED PERSON'S INFORMATION	Name of Restrained Person (Last, First, Middle) SNOOPIE, SAM S.				

Drivers License or ID Number (specify type) 987-6564-12	Nickname SNOOP	Sex M	Race W	Birthdate 5/2/69

Height 5'11"	Weight 160 lbs	Eye Color BLUE	Hair Color BLONDE	Skin Tone FAIR	Build SLIGHT	Relation to Protected Person HUSBAND

Last Known Address (Street, City, State, Zip) 777 N. 1ST AVE, SPOKANE, WA 99202	Home Phone 333-7777	Interpreter Required? NO Language:

Other Address (Street, City, State, Zip), if any:

Employer XYZ CORPORATION	Employer's Address 822 J. STREET, SPOKANE	WORK Hours: 9 am to 5 pm Phone:

Vehicle License Number UNKNOWN	Vehicle Make and Model CHEVROLET CAMARO	Vehicle Color RED	Vehicle Year 1998

PROTECTED PERSON'S INFORMATION	Name of Protected Person (Last, First, Middle) SNOOPIE, SUE O.	

Sex F	Race W	Birthdate 10/02/71

If your information **is not confidential**, enter your address and phone number(s).

Current Address (Street, City, State, Zip)	Phone

If your information **is confidential**, you may provide the name, address and phone number of someone willing to be your "contact."

Contact Name JOAN CLARK	Contact Address 442 10TH STREET, SPOKANE, WA 97001	Contact Phone 665-1234

MINOR'S INFORMATION	Describe the minor's relationship using terms such as: child, grandchild, stepchild, nephew, none. ➡				Minor's Relationship to Protected Person	Minor's Relationship to Restrained Person
Minor's Name (Last, First, Middle)	Sex	Race	Birthdate	Resides With	Person	Person
SNOOPIE, SUSIE Q.	F	W	01/04/93	MOTHER	CHILD	CHILD

HAZARD INFORMATION	Weapons	Guns/Rifles	Knives	Explosives	Other	Location of Weapons:
Describe in detail:						Vehicle ☐ On Person ☐ Residence ☐

CURRENT STATUS (For DV Orders Only)   *(circle)*

		Respondent's History Includes:
Are you and the restrained person living together right now?	Yes No	☐ Mental Health Problems (Commitment, Treatment, Suicide
Does the restrained person know you are trying to get this order?	Yes No	Attempt, Other) ☒ Assault ☐ Assault with Weapons
Does the restrained person know he/she may be moved out of home?	Yes No	☐ Alcohol/Drug Abuse
Is the restrained person likely to react violently when served?	Yes No	

☐ See Reverse For Additional Information   Prepared by: SUE SNOOPIE   Date JAN. 5, 200-

WPF DR 04.0180 LEIS (12/2001)

3

PRELIMINARY NOTES ON PROCEDURE

a. GENERAL

The Administrator for the Courts of Washington State has developed standard *mandatory forms* for people doing their own divorces. Under Washington law, a notary is not needed for your signature on these forms. Mandatory forms have an identifying number (e.g., Form DR 04.0400, Decree of Dissolution). Copies of mandatory forms are available in Self-Counsel's *Divorce Forms for Washington* package, which can be purchased where you bought this book, or you can use the order form at the front of this book. The forms may also be obtained by contacting the clerk of the court for your county or the Administrative Office of the Courts at:

> Administrative Office of the Courts
> 1206 Quince Street SE
> P.O. Box 41170
> Olympia, Washington 98504-1170
> (360) 753-3365

When there is more than one page to a form, staple the pages together in the upper left corner.

b. STYLE OF CAUSE

All legal documents must have a heading known as the "style of cause" so they can be properly identified. Specifically, the style of cause in a divorce action will contain the following information:

(a) Court case number that will be stamped or written on the original

and all copies of the Petition when it is filed and that should be used on all subsequent documents filed

(b) Name of the court

(c) Full names of petitioner and respondent

The style of cause will head *all* of your documents. It is preprinted on the forms. You just have to fill in the information for your case as in Sample 8.

c. FORMAT FOR COURT ORDERS THAT YOU TYPE YOURSELF

If you need to file papers and have no mandatory forms available from the Court Administrator, follow these guidelines. For maximum clarity and legibility, courts prefer that documents be typed.

All pleadings should be on bond paper. The paper must be 8" x 11". Space of approximately four inches at the top of the first page of each document should be left for the clerk's stamp. All other pages should have a two-inch margin at the top and bottom.

The bottom left side of all papers should have the name of the paper (e.g., Petition, Decree, or Findings of Fact), and the page number of the document printed.

Your name should be typed under your signature on each document you sign.

SUPERIOR COURT OF WASHINGTON
COUNTY OF   KING

In Re the Marriage of:

JANE HOOD

Petitioner

and

JOHN HOOD

Respondent

NO: XX-X-XXXXX-X

RESPONSE TO PETITION
(DOMESTIC RELATIONS)
(RSP)

4
STEP-BY-STEP PROCEDURE

a. THE PETITION FOR DISSOLUTION OF MARRIAGE

The first step in obtaining your divorce is to fill out a Petition for Dissolution of Marriage (Form DR 01.0100; see Sample 12). This is the form that requests the Superior Court of Washington to terminate your marriage. The spouse who files the Petition is called the petitioner and the other spouse is called the respondent.

When you fill out the forms, be sure that each section is filled in. The forms have check boxes and you must check the correct box in each case. In some cases this will be the box that says "does not apply." Be sure to check this box if the subject matter does not apply to your case.

The Marriage Dissolution Act requires that your Petition contain the following information:

(a) The date and place of marriage

(b) The date on which the parties separated

(c) A statement saying whether or not the wife is pregnant

(d) A parenting plan (see Sample 15)

(e) A statement as to whether there is community property to be disposed of (and how that property will be disposed of)

(f) A statement of relief sought (This statement should include a request for dissolution of the marriage and, where applicable, residential arrangements for the children; visitation desired; level of child support desired; maintenance requested; division of property; division of the debts; and a request that the property settlement attached to the Petition be approved and incorporated in the Decree of Dissolution.)

Fill out your Petition carefully. Use the example in Sample 12 as a guide, but use your own information and your own words. Be sure to express yourself clearly. If a clause does not apply in your case, cross it out and fill in the particulars of your situation.

In addition to the Petition, you will be required to fill out a Confidential Information Form (Form DRPSCU 09.0200), as shown in Sample 9. If you require more space, you will use the Addendum to Confidential Information Form (Form DRPSCU 09.0210), shown in Sample 10.

The information in these forms will be filed in a separate file that is open only to you, your spouse, your lawyers (if applicable), and certain public officials (primarily those involved with support collection). Of course, the judges considering your case will also have access to this file. Other documents concerning your financial affairs, such as your Financial Statement and tax returns, are also included in this separate, sealed file.

The sealed file has a cover page (Sample 11) on which you should list the documents included. If you do not want your spouse to know where you live, you may delete any information regarding your whereabouts from your documents.

1. When you and your spouse file together

If you and your spouse have both agreed to the divorce and its terms, you may fill out the Petition together and both sign it.

When you and your spouse are cooperating like this, you should attach Form DR 01.0330, Joinder, filled out and signed by your spouse. (See Sample 13.) If your spouse agrees to divorce but does not agree with the terms of your Petition, he or she should file an Acceptance of Service, Form DR 01.0310, Sample 14.

Now that your Petition is filled out and has been signed by you and your spouse, take the original plus two copies to the county courthouse. If children are involved, your Parenting Plan (see Sample 15) should be attached to the Petition.

Pay the filing fee in cash to the cashier at the county clerk's office. The county clerk will place a number on the original and both copies and will stamp all three with the "filed" stamp showing the date you filed the papers.

The 90-day reconciliation period begins on the date stamped on your papers if your spouse has signed a Joinder of the Petition (see Sample 13). (If he or she has not signed, then the 90-day period begins only after your spouse has been served with a Petition and Summons.)

The county clerk will keep the original of your Petition and give you the stamped copies. Whenever you wish to inquire about your file from the county clerk, refer to the number on your copy. The county clerk will also ask you to fill in a vital statistics form required by the Washington State Department of Health. You will need to know your own and your spouse's place and date of birth to complete this form.

2. When you and your spouse are not filing together

If you and your spouse have both signed the Petition for Dissolution, a Summons (Form DR 01.0200) is not necessary and should not be filled out or served. But if your spouse is not cooperating, you should attach a Summons to your Petition. The Summons is a form used to notify your spouse that you have asked the court to terminate your marriage (see Sample 16).

Fill out the Summons at the same time you fill out the Petition. Then staple (in the upper left-hand corner) the Summons on top of the Petition and take both to the county clerk for filing.

Once you have filed the Summons and Petition with the county clerk, both must be served on your spouse. You cannot deliver the Summons and Petition yourself, because the law says that the papers must be served by a person who is not a party to the divorce.

There are three ways you can have the Summons and Petition served on your spouse:

(a) Take the papers to the sheriff of the county in which your spouse lives and pay the service fee.

(b) Look up the name of a process service in the Yellow Pages of your telephone book under the headings "Attorney's Service Bureaus" or "Process Servers" and call them. They will tell you how to hire their services and how much they charge.

(c) Ask a friend 18 years or older to serve it.

If your spouse lives outside the state of Washington, you must still have the Summons and Petition served. Go to the directory library of your telephone company and ask for the telephone book for the city in which your spouse lives. Look up a process server in the Yellow Pages; write to them, giving the address of your spouse and asking what the service charge will be.

Upon receiving a reply, mail the copy of the Summons and Petition, along with the required fee, to the process server in your spouse's city. (If your spouse is missing, or you cannot afford a process server, please see chapter 5, section **a.**) If your spouse lives in another country, you should seek legal advice to have the Summons and Petition served.

Once your spouse has been served the Summons and Petition, the sheriff or the process server will mail you a paper called a Return of Service (Form DR 01.0250). This paper proves that your spouse has been notified of the divorce proceedings (see Sample 17).

If a friend serves the papers, he or she must prepare and sign a Return of Service form. The form is available from the Office of the Administrator for the Courts.

Take the Return of Service to the county clerk's office; it will be placed in your court file. Unless this paper is in your court file (or you and your spouse have both signed the Petition), the court will not sign your Decree of Dissolution, which grants your divorce.

If your spouse does not respond to the Petition within the time set out in the Summons, you may ask the court for an Order of Default and proceed without your spouse's consent after the 90-day reconciliation period has passed. You should do this by filing a Motion and Declaration for Default and an Order of Default. (See Samples 18 and 19.) Count the 90 days from the day your spouse is served.

When you ask for an Order of Default, you must present a declaration that your spouse is not a member of the armed services. See the Motion and Declaration for Default (Sample 18), which contains that declaration, and see section **f.3.** later in this chapter.

b IF YOUR SPOUSE FILES A RESPONSE

If your spouse is served with the Summons and Petition and disagrees with what you have written, he or she may file a Response within the time limit set out in the Summons. This is called contesting the divorce. Your spouse's Response must be made in Form DR 01.0300 (see Sample 20). (If you are the responding party, then you must fill out a copy of the form to respond to a petition.)

The Response is filed by your spouse in the court in which you have begun the action, and a copy is sent to you or your lawyer. The Response sets out the areas of your Petition with which your spouse disagrees. Often the Response is drawn up by a lawyer. If you receive a Response from your spouse, you have two options:

(a) Negotiate the disputed areas with your spouse. If your spouse has an attorney, try to negotiate with him or her and reach some type of agreement. This agreement would form the basis for the next steps in your divorce procedure, namely the Findings of Fact and Decree of Dissolution of Marriage discussed later in this chapter (see section **f.**). Either you or your spouse may prepare these documents based on the agreement you come to. Both these documents must be signed by both parties, either personally or through your respective attorneys.

(b) If you cannot reach an agreement, you should retain a lawyer to represent you. It is generally unwise to attempt to handle a contested case in court by yourself. It is your right, however, to do so. The procedure is this: After your spouse has filed his or her Response, go to the clerk's office and file a Notice of Trial. This notice must be filed with the clerk and served on your spouse or his or her attorney. You must make a sworn declaration that the notice has been mailed to your spouse or his or her attorney or served on one of them. This declaration must also be filed. The system of setting cases for trial varies widely from county to county, so you should ask the clerk or court administrator in charge of such settings how it is done in your county. The wait for a trial date may vary from as little as two months in some of the smaller counties to over a year in the larger ones.

c. OBTAINING TEMPORARY RESTRAINING ORDERS AND RELIEF

If you need to obtain restraining orders during the 90-day waiting period, you should file an Order to Show Cause along with the Petition for Dissolution. To obtain an Order to Show Cause, you first must make your request on a Motion and Declaration for an Order to Show Cause and Order to Show Cause (see Sample 5, Form DR 04.0150 and Sample 6, Form DR 04.0170 in chapter 2 and the accompanying discussion).

The Order to Show Cause (see Sample 6) will order the respondent to come to court on a particular date and answer whether or not he or she agrees with the things that you have asked for. To obtain the order, you must explain to the court, in the Declaration, what you wish the court to do. Use your own words to describe what you want and why you feel the court should order that this be granted.

After you have filled out the Motion and your Declaration and signed it (if you use the declaration form, you do not need to have it notarized), go to the Superior Court and have the judge or commissioner sign the Order to Show Cause. The Motion and Order to Show Cause must then be filed with the county clerk, and a copy of each must be served on your spouse at least eight days before the Motion is to be heard. If you are unable to serve your spouse in time, redo the order by simply writing "Alias" above the words "Order to Show Cause" and having the judge sign a

new Order and assign a new date. Be sure that you serve all of the papers, including the first Order to Show Cause, the alias Order to Show Cause, your Declaration, and your Motion for an Order to Show Cause. Please see section **a.2.** of this chapter for the proper service methods that you must use.

In some counties, you must call the court to confirm that you are in fact proceeding with your Motion. When you file your Motion and Order to Show Cause, check with the clerk of the court to confirm where you must call to confirm, and any time limits for confirming your Motion.

On the day of the hearing, you must appear at the court to argue for the things that you have asked for or the court will simply strike your Motion and you will not get an Order. After the judge has told you what will be granted, then you must prepare the Temporary Order (see Sample 21), sign it, and if your spouse has appeared, have your spouse sign that he or she received a copy. Then ask the judge to sign the Order. If your spouse will not sign the Order, you need a Notice of Motion on which you should write "Note of Presentation" setting a date to present the Order in the form that you have drawn it up to the judge. Serve the Notice of Motion on your spouse by mail, along with a copy of the Order that you will present. You must file an Affidavit of Mailing with the clerk, along with the Notice, and on the day that you have set the hearing, present the Order to the court. Normally the court will sign the Order you have requested, if it is consistent with what the judge feels that he or she has ordered.

d. OBTAINING TEMPORARY ORDERS OTHER THAN RESTRAINING ORDERS

If you wish to obtain temporary orders for—

    (a) a Temporary Parenting Plan (a custody and visitation order),

(b) child support,

(c) an order that entitles you to the temporary use of personal property, or

(d) an order requiring your spouse to pay certain debts,

you must serve a Motion and Declaration for Temporary Order, Form DR 04.0100, on your spouse (see Sample 22), or show a cause as in Sample 5, Form DR 04.0150. You will also have to sign a Note for Dissolution Calendar and have it served on your spouse (see Sample 26).

If you use the Order to Show Cause from Sample 5, it must be signed by a Judge but does not require a calendar note. If you use the motion, Sample 22, the Judge does not sign anything, but a calendar note must be served with your motion and filed with the clerk of the court.

If you are asking for maintenance, child support, or attorney fees, you must file a financial declaration, Sample 23, Form DR 01.0550, whether you use the show cause procedure or the notice and motion procedure. If you are asking the judge to adopt a parenting plan by either procedure, you must fill out, file, and serve the Declaration in Support of Parenting Plan, Form DR 04.0120 (see Sample 24).

When the judge has ordered a temporary parenting plan, Form DR 01.0400 (see Sample 15) is attached to the parenting plan as a separate order. The parenting plan should be filled out and in this case, the box at the top marked "temporary" should be checked.

The Order of Child Support, Form DR 01.0500, (see Sample 25), is always a separate order from the remaining orders. The remaining temporary orders are found in Form DR 04.0250 (see Sample 21).

e. **SETTING A COURT DATE AND PREPARING FOR COURT**

If your spouse does not respond to your Summons and Petition, your divorce is non-contested, and is called a default divorce. You must wait 90 days from filing and service of your Petition before you can appear in court and be granted your Decree of Dissolution. During this 90-day period you should do the following:

(a) Go to the county clerk's office and ask to look at your file. The number stamped on your Petition will help the county clerk find your file. Check to see that all your papers are in the file: Petition, Summons, and Return of Service showing that your spouse has received your Summons. The Return of Service is not necessary if you and your spouse have filed together.

(b) Once you have checked your file, ask the county clerk if any other papers are necessary before you can set a court date. The form for setting a non-contested hearing is Form DR 03.0300, the Note for Dissolution Calendar (see Sample 26).

(c) Now you can ask the county clerk to place your case on the default divorce docket. In some counties, the court administrator and not the county clerk will place your case on the default divorce docket.

(d) Make a note of your court date. Should you miss it, the court will move on to the next case, and you will have to set another date.

Now that your court date has been set, you should prepare yourself for your appearance in court. You may want to ask the county clerk if there are any other default divorce files that you could look at. Reading these other default divorce files will give you an idea of what is expected of you. You should also sit in on some default divorces being heard in court. Ask the county clerk when such divorces are being heard, and whether it is permissible to be present.

f. PREPARING THE FINAL DOCUMENTS

1. Findings of Fact

Although the Findings of Fact and Conclusions of Law, Form DR 04.0300 (see Sample 27), and the Decree of Dissolution, Form DR 04.0400 (see Sample 28) are two separate documents, they are prepared together and contain many of the same provisions.

The Findings of Fact are just what the name implies: the court's findings on the relevant facts concerning the couple's community property, the fitness of one or both parties regarding parenting functions, the distribution of debts, the amount of child support needed, visitation privileges, and so on.

When you are drawing up your Findings of Fact, keep in mind the relief you asked for originally in your Petition. If any changes are made, the court will require your spouse's approval before signing your Findings of Fact and Decree of Dissolution. Therefore, it is a good idea to follow your Petition when filling out your Findings of Fact and your Decree of Dissolution.

In the form, each of the findings is either a plain statement of a fact, such as, "the marital community has the following debts...," or a general statement upon which an order may be based (for example, "The Petitioner is a fit and proper person to have custody of the children of the parties"). It is, in fact, the purpose of the Findings of Fact to state the premises upon which the Decree of Dissolution will be based.

The Conclusions of Law determine that the Decree may legally enter and that the provisions as to residential arrangements for the children, support, maintenance, property, and debt division you have sought are reasonable and legal.

2. The Decree of Dissolution

The Decree, as one might expect, is an order setting out the final terms of the dissolution: what the residential arrangements are for the children; how the community property and community debts shall be distributed between the parties, and, sometimes, certain less common provisions that may have been at issue between the parties, such as who gets to take the income tax deduction for the children, a provision restoring the wife's former name, etc. The Decree must be signed by the judge or court commissioner; it is final and effective at that point.

Essentially, the Decree of Dissolution restates the Findings of Fact in the form of a final court order.

3. Declaration of Non-Military Service or Waiver of Rights Under Soldiers and Sailors' Civil Relief Act and Admission of Service

The Soldiers and Sailors' Civil Relief Act was passed during World War I to protect soldiers and sailors from civil actions brought against them while they were in the military. Therefore, when you, as petitioner, appear in court, you must be able to swear that your spouse, the respondent, is not in the military service or that he or she is in the military but has signed a waiver of rights.

If your spouse is not in the military, you will have to swear to that fact as part of a Motion for Default, Form DR 03.0100. (See Sample 18.)

If your spouse is in the military service, have him or her sign a Waiver of Rights Under the Soldiers and Sailors' Relief Act and Admission of Service before a notary public or judge advocate. (See Sample 29.)

You must bring one or the other of these forms to court with you. If your spouse is in the military and refuses to sign the waiver, you will have to get a lawyer and follow his or her advice before you proceed with your divorce.

Note that if you are a petitioner and in the military service, the Soldiers and Sailors' Civil Relief Act in no way prevents you from bringing an action for divorce. The act merely protects military people from actions against them.

g. APPEARING IN COURT

When you appear in court on the date you have set with the county clerk, you should take a seat and wait for your name to be called. The county clerk will have your file and call your name. When your name is called, walk to the front of the courtroom and take an oath to tell the truth.

You must have with you —

(a) your Findings of Fact and Conclusions of Law, and Decree of Dissolution,

(b) your Acceptance of Service or Joinder (if you and your spouse have filed jointly but your spouse is not appearing with you),

(c) your Declaration of Non-Military Service or Waiver of Rights under Soldiers and Sailors' Civil Relief Act,

(d) your Motion for Default, and Order for Default if your spouse has not responded in the case, and

(e) if there are children, a final Parenting Plan, and an Order of Child Support.

Hand these papers to the bailiff if one is present in the court.

The judge will then motion you to have a seat in the witness box. At this point you may wish to explain that you are representing yourself. You will then testify on the information contained in your Findings of Fact and Decree of Dissolution. You will want to state the following:

(a) Your name and address

(b) Whom you were mar

(c) When and where you

(d) That either, or both, resident in Washing Petition was filed

(e) That your marriage has irretrievably broken and you can no longer live as husband and wife

(f) That you request the court to terminate your marriage

You would then go on to state how you want the court to settle such matters as matrimonial property and access to the children (naturally this would follow the relief sought in your Petition). For example:

> We have X number of children of the marriage. Their names and birthdays are _____.
> We have agreed on residential arrangements for the children.
>
> and/or
>
> We have _____ as our debts. Our assets are
> _____.
>
> We have agreed that our debts shall be paid by X. Our assets shall be divided as follows
> _____.

These are just rough examples of what you would be expected to say. Before you go to court, you should sit down with a copy of your Petition or your Findings of Fact and draw up brief statements covering each area of relief sought. Then, when you are in court, you can use these notes as a reminder to yourself about what you want to say next. It is not a good idea to read directly from your notes.

The judge will ask you any questions he or she may feel you missed, and then will sign your Decree of Dissolution. You can then thank the court and step down from the witness box.

Now you should take the copies of the papers you brought to court to the county clerk's office. The county clerk will stamp these copies as filed and then will affix the stamp of the judge who signed the originals. In this way you have duplicates of the papers on file in the court. And you have your divorce!

CONFIDENTIAL INFORMATION FORM (INFO)

Do not file in a	County: SPOKANE	Cause Number: XX-X-XXXXX-X
public access file.	**COURT CLERK: THIS IS A RESTRICTED ACCESS DOCUMENT**	

☒ Divorce/Separation/Invalidity/Nonparental Custody/Paternity/Modifications ☐ Other

☐ Domestic Violence ☐ Antiharassment ☐ Information Change (Check if you are updating information)

☐ **A restraining order or protection order is in effect protecting** ☒ **the petitioner** ☐ **the respondent** ☒ **the children.**

☒ **The health, safety, or liberty of a party or child would be jeopardized by disclosure of address information because:** THE RESPONDENT HAS BEEN PHYSICALLY VIOLENT TOWARD THE PETITIONER IN THE PAST.

The following information about the parties is required in all cases:.
(Use the Addendum To Confidential Information Form to list additional parties or children)

Petitioner Information .			Type or Print only	Respondent Information		
Name (Last, First, Middle) SNOOPIE, SUE O.				**Name (Last, first, Middle)** SNOOPIE, SAM S.		
Race W	Sex F	Birthdate 10/02/71		Race W	Sex M	Birthdate 5/2/69
Drivers Lic. or Identicard (# and State) SPOKANE 1234-5678				**Drivers Lic. or Identicard (# and State), (or, if unavailable, residential address)** SPOKANE 987-6564-12		
Mailing Address (P.O.Box/Street, City, State, Zip) 333 HOMESTEAD AVE., SPOKANE, WA 98211				**Mailing Address (P.O.Box/Street, City, State, Zip)** 777 N. 1ST AVE., SPOKANE, WA 99202		

The following information is required if there are children involved in the proceeding.
(Soc. Sec. No. is not required for petitions in protection order cases (Domestic Violence/Antiharassment).

Child's Name (Last, First, Middle)	1 SNOOPIE, SUSIE Q.
Child's Race/Sex/Birthdate	W/F/01/04/93
Child's Soc. Sec. No. (If required)	
Child's Present Address or Whereabouts	333 HOMESTEAD AVE., SPOKANE, WA 98211

Child's Name (Last, First, Middle)	2
Child's Race/Sex/Birthdate	
Child's Soc. Sec. No. (If required)	
Child's Present Address or Whereabouts	

List the names and present addresses of the persons with whom the child(ren) lived during the last five years:

SUE SNOOPY, 333 HOMESTEAD AVE., SPOKANE, WA

SAM SNOOPY, 777 N. 1ST AVE., SPOKANE, WA

List the names and present addresses of any person besides you and the respondent who has physical custody of, or claims rights of custody or visitation with, the child(ren):

NONE

Except for petitions in protection order cases (Domestic Violence/Antiharassment), the following **information is required:**

Petitioner's Information	Respondent's Information
Soc. Sec. No.: 222-234-456	Soc. Sec. No.: 333-345-567
Residential Address (Street, City, State, Zip) 333 HOMESTEAD AVE., SPOKANE, WA 98211	Residential Address (Street, City, State, Zip) 777 N. 1ST AVE., SPOKANE, WA 99202
Telephone No.: (313) 888-9991	Telephone No.: (313) 333-7777
Employer: DOUGHBOY BAKERY	Employer: XYZ CORPORATION
Empl. Address: 333 YEAST LANE, SPOKANE, WA	Empl. Address: 822 J. STREET, SPOKANE, WA
Empl. Phone No.: (313) 887-2222	Empl. Phone No.: (313) 555-5555

Additional information:_____
_____
_____
_____

☐ Addendum To Confidential Information Form is attached.

I certify under penalty of perjury under the laws of the state of Washington that the above information is true and accurate concerning myself and is accurate to the best of my knowledge as to the other party, or is unavailable. The information is unavailable because _____
_____.

Signed on JANUARY 5, 200-   (Date) at   SPOKANE, WASHINGTON_____   (City and State).

*Sue Snoopie*_____
Petitioner/~~Respondent~~

ADDENDUM TO CONFIDENTIAL INFORMATION FORM

ADDENDUM TO CONFIDENTIAL INFORMATION FORM (AD)		
Do not file in a public access file.	County:	Cause Number:
	COURT CLERK: THIS IS A RESTRICTED ACCESS DOCUMENT	

The following information about additional parties is required in all cases.

Additional Petitioner Information	Type or Print only	Additional Respondent Information
Name (Last, First, Middle)		Name (Last, first, Middle)

Race	Sex	Birthdate	Race	Sex	Birthdate

Drivers Lic. or Identicard (# and State)	Drivers Lic. or Identicard (# and State), (or, if unavailable, residential address)

Mailing Address (P.O.Box/Street, City, State, Zip)	Mailing Address (P.O.Box/Street, City, State, Zip)

The following information is required if there are additional children involved in the proceeding
(Soc. Sec. No. is not required for petitions in protection order cases (Domestic Violence/Antiharassment).

Child's Name (Last, First, Middle)	3
Child's Race/Sex/Birthdate	
Child's Soc. Sec. No. (If required)	
Child's Present Address or Whereabouts	
Child's Name (Last, First, Middle)	4
Child's Race/Sex/Birthdate	
Child's Soc. Sec. No. (If required)	
Child's Present Address or Whereabouts	

Except for petitions in protection order cases (Domestic Violence/Antiharassment), the following information **is required:**

Additional Petitioner Information	Additional Respondent Information
Soc. Sec. No.:	Soc. Sec. No.:
Residential Address (Street, City, State, Zip)	Residential Address (Street, City, State, Zip)
Telephone No.: ( )	Telephone No.: ( )
Employer:	Employer:
Empl. Address:	Empl. Address:
Empl. Phone No.: ( )	Empl. Phone No.: ( )

CONF INFO FORM ADDENDUM (AD) - Page 1 of 1
WPF DRPSCU 09.0210 (9/2001) RCW 26.23.050

SELF-COUNSEL PRESS – DIV WA (B-1) 01

SUPERIOR COURT OF WASHINGTON
COUNTY OF SPOKANE

In re:

SUSIE SNOOPIE	Child(ren),	**NO.** XX-X-XXXXX-X
SUE SNOOPIE	Petitioner(s),	**SEALED FINANCIAL SOURCE DOCUMENTS**
and		**(SEALFN)**
SAM SNOOPIE	Respondent(s).	**CLERK'S ACTION REQUIRED**

SEALED FINANCIAL SOURCE DOCUMENTS

(List documents below and write "Sealed" at least one inch from the top of the first page of each document.)

[X] Income Tax records.
Period Covered: 200-, 200-

[   ] Bank statements.
Period Covered:

[X] Pay Stubs.
Period Covered: JUNE 200- TO NOVEMBER 200-

[   ] Credit Card Statements.
Period Covered:

[   ] Other:

Submitted by:

Sue Snoopie   PETITIONER PRO SE

NOTICE: The other party will have access to these financial source documents. If you are concerned for your safety or the safety of the children, you may redact (block out or delete) information that identifies your location.

SUPERIOR COURT OF WASHINGTON
COUNTY OF SPOKANE

In re the Marriage of:

SUE SNOOPIE

                                        Petitioner,

and

SAM SNOOPIE

                                        Respondent.

NO. XX-X-XXXXX-X

PETITION FOR DISSOLUTION
OF MARRIAGE
(PTDSS)

I. BASIS

1.1   IDENTIFICATION OF PETITIONER.

Name (first/last) ___SUE SNOOPIE_____. Birth date ___6/3/70_____

Last known residence ___SPOKANE, WASHINGTON_____ (county and state).

1.2   IDENTIFICATION OF RESPONDENT.

Name (first/last) ___SAM SNOOPIE_____, Birth date ___5/2/69_____

Last known residence ___SPOKANE, WASHINGTON_____ (county and state).

1.3   CHILDREN OF THE MARRIAGE DEPENDENT UPON EITHER OR BOTH SPOUSES.

Name (first/last) ___SUSIE SNOOPIE_____ Age ___10_____

Name (first/last) _____ Age _____

Name (first/last) _____ Age _____

Name (first/last) _____ Age _____

Name (first/last) _____ Age _____

Name (first/last) _____ Age _____

1.4   ALLEGATION REGARDING MARRIAGE.

This marriage is irretrievably broken.

1.5   DATE AND PLACE OF MARRIAGE.

The parties were married on ___JULY 2, 1980___ at ___SEATTLE, WASHINGTON___.
                                     [Date]   [Place]

1.6   SEPARATION.

[ ]   Husband and wife are not separated.
[X]   Husband and wife separated on ___MARCH 1, 200-___.
                                                     [Date]

1.7   JURISDICTION.

This court has jurisdiction over the marriage.

[X]   This court has jurisdiction over the respondent because:
      [X]   the respondent is presently residing in Washington.
      [ ]   the petitioner and respondent lived in Washington during their marriage and the petitioner continues to reside, or be a member of the armed forces stationed, in this state.
      [ ]   the petitioner and respondent may have conceived a child while within Washington.
      [ ]   Other:

[ ]   This court does not have jurisdiction over the respondent.

1.8   PROPERTY.

There is community or separate property owned by the parties. The court should make a fair and equitable division of all the property.

[ ]   The division of property should be determined by the court at a later date.

[X]   The petitioner's recommendation for the division of property is set forth below.

      [X]   The petitioner should be awarded the parties' interest in the following property:

A house at North 123 Beagle Street, Spokane, Washington

1998 Taurus car

Her bank accounts

The furniture in the family home

Her pension at Acme Widget Co.

PET FOR DISSO OF MARRIAGE (PTDSS) - Page 2 of 7
WPF DR 01.0100 (9/2001) - RCW 26.09.020
              SELF-COUNSEL PRESS – DIV WA (1-2) 01

60

⊠   The respondent should be awarded the parties' interest in the following property:

His pension at XYZ Corp.

1999 Buick

His bank account

[ ]   Other:

1.9   DEBTS AND LIABILITIES.

[ ]   The parties have no debts and liabilities.
⊠   The parties have debts and liabilities. The court should make a fair and equitable division of all debts and liabilities.

     [ ]   The division of debts and liabilities should be determined by the court at a later date.
     ⊠   The petitioner's recommendation for the division of debts and liabilities is set forth below.

         ⊠   The petitioner should be ordered to pay the following debts and liabilities to the following creditors:

            Nordstrom $500

            Mastercard $200

         ⊠   The respondent should be ordered to pay the following debts and liabilities to the following creditors:

            Visa $2,000

            Credit Union Loan $1,000

         [ ]   Other:

SAMPLE 12—Continued

1.10   SPOUSAL MAINTENANCE.

       [X]   Spousal maintenance should not be ordered.
       [ ]   There is a need for spousal maintenance as follows:

       [ ]   Other:

1.11   CONTINUING RESTRAINING ORDER.

       [X]   Does not apply.
       [ ]   A continuing restraining order should be entered which restrains or enjoins the respondent from assaulting, harassing, molesting or disturbing the peace of the petitioner.
       [ ]   A continuing restraining order should be entered which restrains or enjoins the respondent from going onto the grounds of or entering the home, work place or school of the petitioner or the day care or school of the following children:
             _____
       [ ]   A continuing restraining order should be entered which restrains or enjoins the respondent from knowingly coming within or knowingly remaining within _____ (distance) of the home, work place or school of the petitioner or the day care or school of these children:
             _____
             Other: _____.

       [ ]   Other:

1.12   PREGNANCY.

       [X]   The wife is not pregnant.
       [ ]   The wife is pregnant. The father of the unborn child is [ ] the husband [ ] not the husband [ ] unknown.

1.13   JURISDICTION OVER THE CHILDREN.

       [ ]   Does not apply because there are no dependent children.
       [X]   This court has jurisdiction over the children for the reasons set forth below.

       [ ]   This court has exclusive continuing jurisdiction. The court has previously made a child custody, parenting plan, residential schedule or visitation determination in this matter and retains jurisdiction under RCW 26.27.211.

       [X]   This state is the home state of the children because

             [X]   the children lived in Washington with a parent or a person acting as a parent for at least six consecutive months immediately preceding the commencement of this proceeding.

62

[ ]   the children are less than six months old and have lived in Washington with a parent or a person acting as parent since birth.

[ ]   any absences from Washington have been only temporary.

[ ]   Washington was the home state of the children within six months before the commencement of this proceeding and the children are absent from the state but a parent or person acting as a parent continued to live in this state.

[ ]   The children and the parents or the children and at least one parent or person acting as a parent, have significant connection with the state other than mere physical presence; and substantial evidence is available in this state concerning the children's care, protection, training and personal relationships; and

[ ]   the children have no home state elsewhere.

[ ]   the children's home state has declined to exercise jurisdiction on the ground that this state is the more appropriate forum under RCW 26.27.261 or .271.

[ ]   All courts in the children's home state have declined to exercise jurisdiction on the ground that a court of this state is the more appropriate forum to determine the custody of the children under RCW 26.27.261 or .271.

[ ]   No other state has jurisdiction.

[ ]   This court has temporary emergency jurisdiction over this proceeding because the children are present in this state and the children have been abandoned or it is necessary in an emergency to protect the children because the children, or a sibling or parent of the children is subjected to or threatened with abuse. RCW 26.27.231.

[ ]   Other:

1.14   CHILD SUPPORT AND PARENTING PLAN FOR DEPENDENT CHILDREN.

[ ]   The parties have no dependent children.

[X]   Support for the dependent children listed in paragraph 1.3, above, should be set pursuant to the Washington State Child Support Schedule.

Name of Child	Mother's Name	Father's Name
SUSIE SNOOPIE	SUE SNOOPIE	SAM SNOOPIE

SAMPLE 12—Continued

The petitioner's proposed parenting plan for these children:

☒   is attached and is incorporated by reference as part of this Petition.
[ ]   will be filed and served at a later date pursuant to RCW 26.09.181.

(The following information is required only for those children who are included in the petitioner's proposed parenting plan.)

During the last five years, the children have lived:

☒   in no place other than the state of Washington and with no person other than the petitioner or the respondent.
[ ]   in the following places with the following persons (list each place the children lived, including the state of Washington, the dates the children lived there and the names of the persons with whom the children lived. The present addresses of those persons must be listed in the required Confidential Information Form):

Claims to custody or visitation;

☒   The petitioner does not know of any person other than the respondent who has physical custody of, or claims to have custody or visitation rights to, the children.
[ ]   The following persons have physical custody of, or claim to have custody or visitation rights to the children (list their names and the children concerned below and list their present addresses in the Confidential Information Form. Do not list the responding party):

Involvement in any other proceeding concerning the children;

☒   The petitioner has not been involved in any other proceeding regarding the children.
[ ]   The petitioner has been involved in the following proceedings regarding the children (list the court, the case number, and the date of the judgment or order):

Other legal proceedings concerning the children.

☒   The petitioner does not know of any other legal proceedings concerning the children.
[ ]   The petitioner knows of the following legal proceedings which concern the children (list the children concerned, the court, the case number, and the kind of proceeding):

1.15   OTHER.

II. RELIEF REQUESTED

The petitioner REQUESTS the court to enter a decree of dissolution and to grant the relief below.

[ ]   Provide reasonable maintenance for the [ ] husband [ ] wife.

[X]   Approve the petitioner's proposed parenting plan for the dependent children.

[X]   Determine support for the dependent children pursuant to the Washington State Child Support Schedule.

[ ]   Approve the separation agreement.

[X]   Divide the property and liabilities.

[X]   Change name of wife to: __SUE SMITH__.

[ ]   Change name of husband to: _____.

[ ]   Enter a continuing restraining order.

[ ]   Order payment of day care expenses for the children.

[X]   Award the tax exemptions for the dependent children as follows:

       TO THE WIFE

[X]   Order payment of attorney's fees, other professional fees and costs.

[ ]   Other:

Dated: __JANUARY 10, 200-__

Sue Snoopie
Signature of Lawyer or Petitioner

__SUE SNOOPIE__
Print or Type Name

I declare under penalty of perjury under the laws of the state of Washington that the foregoing is true and correct.

Signed at ___SPOKANE, WASHINGTON___ on ___JANUARY 10, 200-___
          [Place]   [Date]

Sue Snoopie
Signature

__SUE SNOOPIE__
Print or Type Name

[ ]   JOINDER.

The respondent joins in the petition. By joining in the petition, the respondent agrees to the entry of a decree in accordance with the petition, without further notice.

Dated: _____

_____
Signature of Respondent

__SAM SNOOPIE__
Print or Type Name

SAMPLE 13
JOINDER

SUPERIOR COURT OF WASHINGTON
COUNTY OF SPOKANE

In re the Marriage of:

SUE SNOOPIE

Petitioner,	NO. XX-X-XXXXX-X
and	JOINDER
(JN)
SAM SNOOPIE	
Respondent.	

1. JOINDER.

I have read the petition and join in it. I understand that by joining in the petition, a decree may be entered in accordance with the relief requested in the petition, unless prior to the entry of the decree a response is filed and served.

2. NOTICE OF FURTHER PROCEEDINGS.

[ ]   Does not apply.
[X]   I demand notice of all further proceedings in this matter. Further notice should be sent to the following service address: [You may list an address that is not your residential address where you agree to accept legal documents.]

EAST 6000-14TH AVENUE, YAKIMA, WASHINGTON, 98093

3. OTHER.

Dated: JANUARY 10, 200-   *Sam Snoopie*
                                                                         Signature of Joining Party

                                                                         SAM SNOOPIE
                                                                         Print or Type Name

SUPERIOR COURT OF WASHINGTON
COUNTY OF   SPOKANE

In re the Marriage of:

SUE SNOOPIE

                              Petitioner,

and

SAM SNOOPIE

                              Respondent.

NO.   XX-X-XXXXX-X

ACCEPTANCE OF SERVICE
(ACSR)

1.   ACCEPTANCE OF SERVICE.

      __SAM SNOOPIE__   [Name] accepts service of:

      [X] the summons and petition in this action.   [X] a proposed parenting plan.
      [ ] a proposed order of child support.   [X] a financial declaration.
      [ ] proposed Child Support Worksheets.   [ ] other:

2.   CONSENT TO PERSONAL JURISDICTION.

      [X] Does not apply.
      [ ] _____ [Name] consents to personal jurisdiction.
      [ ] Other

3.   OTHER:

Dated: __JANUARY 10, 200-__

Sam Snoopie
Signature of Lawyer or Party Accepting Service

SAM SNOOPIE
Print or Type Name
Notice to party: You may list an address that is not your
residential address where you agree to accept legal documents.

EAST 600-14TH AVENUE
[Address]
YAKIMA, WASHINGTON 98093

SUPERIOR COURT OF WASHINGTON
COUNTY OF SPOKANE

In re the Marriage of:
 	
SUE SNOOPIE
 	
                        Petitioner,
and
 	
SAM SNOOPIE
 	
                        Respondent.
	NO. XX-X-XXXXX-X
	
	PARENTING PLAN
	[ ] PROPOSED **(PPP)**
	[ ] TEMPORARY **(PPT)**
	[X] FINAL ORDER **(PP)**

This parenting plan is:

[X]   the final parenting plan signed by the court pursuant to a decree of dissolution entered on
        MAY 10, 200- [Date].

[ ]   the final parenting plan signed by the court pursuant to an order entered on _____ [Date] which
        modifies a previous parenting plan or custody decree.

[ ]   a temporary parenting plan signed by the court.

[ ]   proposed by _____ [Name].

IT IS HEREBY ORDERED, ADJUDGED AND DECREED:

I. GENERAL INFORMATION

This parenting plan applies to the following children:

Name	Age
SUSIE SNOOPIE	10

II. BASIS FOR RESTRICTIONS

Under certain circumstances, as outlined below, the court may limit or prohibit a parent's contact with the child(ren) and the right to make decisions for the child(ren).

2.1   PARENTAL CONDUCT (RCW 26.09.191(1), (2)).

      [X]   Does not apply.

      [ ]   The [ ] mother's [ ] father's residential time with the child(ren) shall be limited or restrained completely, and mutual decision-making and designation of a dispute resolution process other than court action shall not be required, because [ ] this parent [ ] a person residing with this parent has engaged in the conduct which follows.

            [ ]   Willful abandonment that continues for an extended period of time or substantial refusal to perform parenting functions (this applies only to parents, not to a person who resides with a parent).

            [ ]   Physical, sexual or a pattern of emotional abuse of a child.

            [ ]   A history of acts of domestic violence as defined in RCW 26.50.010(1) or an assault or sexual assault which causes grievous bodily harm or the fear of such harm.

2.2   OTHER FACTORS (RCW 26.09.191(3)).

      [X]   Does not apply.

      [ ]   The [ ] mother's [ ] father's involvement or conduct may have an adverse effect on the child(ren)'s best interests because of the existence of the factors which follow.

            [ ]   Neglect or substantial nonperformance of parenting functions.

            [ ]   A long-term emotional or physical impairment which interferes with the performance of parenting functions as defined in RCW 26.09.004.

            [ ]   A long-term impairment resulting from drug, alcohol, or other substance abuse that interferes with the performance of parenting functions.

            [ ]   The absence or substantial impairment of emotional ties between the parent and child.

            [ ]   The abusive use of conflict by the parent which creates the danger of serious damage to the child's psychological development.

            [ ]   A parent has withheld from the other parent access to the child for a protracted period without good cause.

            [ ]   Other:

III. RESIDENTIAL SCHEDULE

The residential schedule must set forth where the child(ren) shall reside each day of the year, including provisions for holidays, birthdays of family members, vacations, and other special occasions, and what contact the child(ren) shall have with each parent. Parents are encouraged to create a residential schedule that meets the developmental needs of the child(ren) and individual needs of their family. Paragraphs 3.1 through 3.9 are one way to write your residential schedule. If you do not use these paragraphs, write in your own schedule in Paragraph 3.13.

3.1   SCHEDULE FOR CHILDREN UNDER SCHOOL AGE

    ☒   There are no children under school age.

    [ ]   Prior to enrollment in school, the child(ren) shall reside with the [ ] mother [ ] father, except for the following days and times when the child(ren) will reside with or be with the other parent:

from _____ [day and time] to _____ [day and time]

    [ ]   every week [ ] every other week [ ] the first and third week of the month
    [ ]   the second and fourth week of the month [ ] other:

from _____ [day and time] to _____ [day and time]

    [ ]   every week [ ] every other week [ ] the first and third week of the month
    [ ]   the second and fourth week of the month [ ] other:

3.2   SCHOOL SCHEDULE.

Upon enrollment in school, the child(ren) shall reside with the ☒ mother [ ] father, except for the following days and times when the child(ren) will reside with or be with the other parent:

from _Friday, 6 p.m._____ [day and time] to _Sunday, 6 p.m._ [day and time]

    [ ]   every week ☒ every other week [ ] the first and third week of the month
    [ ]   the second and fourth week of the month [ ] other:

from _____ [day and time] to _____ [day and time]

    [ ]   every week [ ] every other week [ ] the first and third week of the month
    [ ]   the second and fourth week of the month [ ] other:

    [ ]   The school schedule will start when each child begins [ ] kindergarten [ ] first grade
           [ ] other:

3.3   SCHEDULE FOR WINTER VACATION.

The child(ren) shall reside with the ☒ mother [ ] father during winter vacation, except for the following days and times when the child(ren) will reside with or be with the other parent:

Winter vacation will be divided with the mother having the child the first part until 9 a.m. on December 25th and the father having the child from December 25th at 9 a.m. until December 31st at 6 p.m.

SAMPLE 15—Continued

3.4   SCHEDULE FOR SPRING VACATION.

The child(ren) shall reside with the [X] mother [ ] father during spring vacation, except for the following days and times when the child(ren) will reside with or be with the other parent:

   The parents will alternate spring vacation. The mother will have even numbered years and the father odd.

3.5   SUMMER SCHEDULE.

Upon completion of the school year, the child(ren) shall reside with the [ ] mother [ ] father, except for the following days and times when the child(ren) will reside with or be with the other parent:

[ ]   Same as school year schedule.
[X]   Other:

   Father shall have the child with him for the month of July.

3.6   VACATION WITH PARENTS.

[ ]   Does not apply.
[X]   The schedule for vacation with parents is as follows:

   Each parent will have two uninterrupted weeks each year for travel. Father will take his two weeks in July.

3.7   SCHEDULE FOR HOLIDAYS.

The residential schedule for the child(ren) for the holidays listed below is as follows:

	With Mother (Specify Year Odd/Even/Every)	With Father (Specify Year Odd/Even/Every)
New Year's Day	Even	Odd
Martin Luther King Day	Odd	Even
Presidents' Day	Even	Odd
Memorial Day	Odd	Even
July 4th	Even	Odd
Labor Day	Odd	Even
Veterans' Day	Even	Odd
Thanksgiving Day	Odd	Even
Christmas Eve	Even	Odd
Christmas Day	Odd	Even

[X]   For purposes of this parenting plan, a holiday shall begin and end as follows (set forth times):

10:00 a.m. to 8:00 p.m.

[ ]   Holidays which fall on a Friday or a Monday shall include Saturday and Sunday.

[ ]   Other:

3.8   SCHEDULE FOR SPECIAL OCCASIONS.

The residential schedule for the child(ren) for the following special occasions (for example, birthdays) is as follows:

	With Mother (Specify Year Odd/Even/Every)	With Father (Specify Year Odd/Even/Every)
Mother's Day	Every	
Father's Day		Every
Mother's Birthday	Every	
Father's Birthday		Every

[ ]   Other:

3.9   PRIORITIES UNDER THE RESIDENTIAL SCHEDULE.

[X]   Does not apply.

[ ]   If the residential schedule, paragraphs 3.1 - 3.8, results in a conflict where the children are scheduled to be with both parents at the same time, the conflict shall be resolved by priority being given as follows:

     [ ]   Rank the order of priority, with 1 being given the highest priority:

         ____ school schedule (3.1, 3.2)   ____ vacation with parents (3.6)
         ____ winter vacation (3.3)   ____ holidays (3.7)
         ____ spring vacation (3.4)   ____ special occasions (3.8)
         ____ summer schedule (3.5)

     [ ]   Other:

3.10   RESTRICTIONS.

[X]   Does not apply because there are no limiting factors in paragraphs 2.1 or 2.2.

[ ]   The [ ] mother's [ ] father's residential time with the children shall be limited because there are limiting factors in paragraphs 2.1 and 2.2. The following restrictions shall apply when the children spend time with this parent:

PARENTING PLAN (PPP, PPT, PP) - Page 5 of 10
WPF DR 01.0400 (9/2001) - RCW 26.09.181; .187; .194   SELF-COUNSEL PRESS – DIV WA (21-5) 01

72

[ ]   There are limiting factors in paragraph 2.2, but there are no restrictions on the
[ ] mother's [ ] father's residential time with the children for the following reasons:

3.11   TRANSPORTATION ARRANGEMENTS.

[ ]   Transportation costs are included in the Child Support Worksheets and/or the Order of Child
Support and should not be included here.

☒   Transportation arrangements for the child(ren), between parents shall be as follows:

      Equally shared.

3.12   DESIGNATION OF CUSTODIAN.

The children named in this parenting plan are scheduled to reside the majority of the time with the [ ]
mother [ ] father. This parent is designated the custodian of the child(ren) solely for purposes of all other
state and federal statutes which require a designation or determination of custody. This designation shall
not affect either parent's rights and responsibilities under this parenting plan.

3.13   OTHER.

3.14   SUMMARY OF RCW 26.09.430 - .480, REGARDING RELOCATION OF A CHILD.

This is a summary only. For the full text, please see RCW 26.09.430 through 26.09.480.

If the person with whom the child resides a majority of the time plans to move, that person shall give notice to every person entitled to court ordered time with the child.

If the move is outside the child's school district, the relocating person must give notice by personal service or by mail requiring a return receipt. This notice must be at least 60 days before the intended move. If the relocating person could not have known about the move in time to give 60 days' notice, that person must give notice within 5 days after learning of the move. The notice must contain the information required in RCW 26.09.440. See also form DRPSCU 07.0500, (Notice of Intended Relocation of A Child).

If the move is within the same school district, the relocating person must provide actual notice by any reasonable means. A person entitled to time with the child may not object to the move but may ask for modification under RCW 26.09.260.

Notice may be delayed for 21 days if the relocating person is entering a domestic violence shelter or is moving to avoid a clear, immediate and unreasonable risk to health and safety.

If information is protected under a court order or the address confidentiality program, it may be withheld from the notice.

A relocating person may ask the court to waive any notice requirements that may put the health and safety of a person or a child at risk.

Failure to give the required notice may be grounds for sanctions, including contempt.

If no objection is filed within 30 days after service of the notice of intended relocation, the relocation will be permitted and the proposed revised residential schedule may be confirmed.

A person entitled to time with a child under a court order can file an objection to the child's relocation whether or not he or she received proper notice.

An objection may be filed by using the mandatory pattern form WPF DRPSCU 07.0700, (Objection to Relocation/Petition for Modification of Custody Decree/Parenting Plan/Residential Schedule). The objection must be served on all persons entitled to time with the child.

The relocating person shall not move the child during the time for objection unless: (a) the delayed notice provisions apply; or (b) a court order allows the move.

If the objecting person schedules a hearing for a date within 15 days of timely service of the objection, the relocating person shall not move the child before the hearing unless there is a clear, immediate and unreasonable risk to the health or safety of a person or a child.

IV. DECISION MAKING

4.1   DAY-TO-DAY DECISIONS.

Each parent shall make decisions regarding the day-to-day care and control of each child while the child is residing with that parent. Regardless of the allocation of decision making in this parenting plan, either parent may make emergency decisions affecting the health or safety of the children.

4.2   MAJOR DECISIONS.

Major decisions regarding each child shall be made as follows:

Education decisions   [ ] mother   [ ] father   ☒ joint

PARENTING PLAN (PPP, PPT, PP) - Page 7 of 10
WPF DR 01.0400 (9/2001) - RCW 26.09.181, .187; .194   SELF-COUNSEL PRESS – DIV WA (21-7) 01

74

SAMPLE 15—Continued

Non-emergency health care	[ ]	mother	[ ]	father	[X]	joint
Religious upbringing	[ ]	mother	[ ]	father	[X]	joint
_____	[ ]	mother	[ ]	father	[ ]	joint
_____	[ ]	mother	[ ]	father	[ ]	joint
_____	[ ]	mother	[ ]	father	[ ]	joint
_____	[ ]	mother	[ ]	father	[ ]	joint
_____	[ ]	mother	[ ]	father	[ ]	joint
_____	[ ]	mother	[ ]	father	[ ]	joint

4.3   RESTRICTIONS IN DECISION MAKING.

[X]   Does not apply because there are no limiting factors in paragraphs 2.1 and 2.2 above.
[ ]   Sole decision making shall be ordered to the [ ] mother [ ] father for the following reasons:

    [ ]   A limitation on the other parent's decision making authority is mandated by RCW 26.09.191 (See paragraph 2.1).
    [ ]   Both parents are opposed to mutual decision making.
    [ ]   One parent is opposed to mutual decision making, and such opposition is reasonably based on the following criteria:

        (a)   The existence of a limitation under RCW 26.09.191;
        (b)   The history of participation of each parent in decision making in each of the areas in RCW 26.09.184(4)(a);
        (c)   Whether the parents have demonstrated ability and desire to cooperate with one another in decision making in each of the areas in RCW 26.09.184(4)(a); and
        (d)   The parents' geographic proximity to one another, to the extent that it affects their ability to make timely mutual decisions.

[ ]   There are limiting factors in paragraph 2.2, but there are no restrictions on mutual decision making for the following reasons:

V. DISPUTE RESOLUTION

The purpose of this dispute resolution process is to resolve disagreements about carrying out this parenting plan. This dispute resolution process may, and under some local court rules or the provisions of this plan must, be used before filing a petition to modify the plan or a motion for contempt for failing to follow the plan.

[X]   Disputes between the parties, other than child support disputes, shall be submitted to (list person or agency):

    [ ]   counseling by   _____, or

    [X]   mediation by   __ABC Mediation Services_____, or

    [ ]   arbitration by   _____.

PARENTING PLAN (PPP, PPT, PP) - Page 8 of 10
WPF DR 01.0400 (9/2001) – RCW 26.09.181; .187; .194

SELF-COUNSEL PRESS – DIV WA (21-8) 01

The cost of this process shall be allocated between the parties as follows:

[ ]   _____% mother _____% father.
[X]   based on each party's proportional share of income from line 6 of the child support worksheets.
[ ]   as determined in the dispute resolution process.

The counseling, mediation or arbitration process shall be commenced by notifying the other party by [X] written request [ ] certified mail [ ] other:

In the dispute resolution process:

(a)   Preference shall be given to carrying out this Parenting Plan.
(b)   Unless an emergency exists, the parents shall use the designated process to resolve disputes relating to implementation of the plan, except those related to financial support.
(c)   A written record shall be prepared of any agreement reached in counseling or mediation and of each arbitration award and shall be provided to each party.
(d)   If the court finds that a parent has used or frustrated the dispute resolution process without good reason, the court shall award attorneys' fees and financial sanctions to the other parent.
(e)   The parties have the right of review from the dispute resolution process to the superior court.

[ ]   No dispute resolution process, except court action is ordered.

VI. OTHER PROVISIONS

[X]   There are no other provisions.
[ ]   There are the following other provisions:

VII. DECLARATION FOR PROPOSED PARENTING PLAN

[ ]   Does not apply.
[X]   (Only sign if this is a proposed parenting plan.) I declare under penalty of perjury under the laws of the state of Washington that this plan has been proposed in good faith and that the statements in Part II of this Plan are true and correct.

PARENTING PLAN (PPP, PPT, PP) - Page 9 of 10
WPF DR 01.0400 (9/2001) - RCW 26.09.181, .187; .194   SELF-COUNSEL PRESS – DIV WA (21-9) 01

76

Sue Snoopie
_____
Mother

04/30/200-, SPOKANE, WA
_____
Date and Place of Signature

Sam Snoopie
_____
Father

04/30/200-, SPOKANE, WA
_____
Date and Place of Signature

VIII. ORDER BY THE COURT

It is ordered, adjudged and decreed that the parenting plan set forth above is adopted and approved as an order of this court.

WARNING: Violation of residential provisions of this order with actual knowledge of its terms is punishable by contempt of court and may be a criminal offense under RCW 9A.040.060(2) or 9A.40.070(2). Violation of this order may subject a violator to arrest.

When mutual decision making is designated but cannot be achieved, the parties shall make a good faith effort to resolve the issue through the dispute resolution process.

If a parent fails to comply with a provision of this plan, the other parent's obligations under the plan are not affected.

Dated: ___05/10/200-_____

I.M. Judge
_____
JUDGE/COMMISSIONER

Presented by:

Approved for entry:

Sue Snoopie
_____
Signature

SUE SNOOPIE
_____
Print or Type Name

Sam Snoopie
_____
Signature

SAM SNOOPIE
_____
Print or Type Name

SAMPLE 16
SUMMONS

SUPERIOR COURT OF WASHINGTON
COUNTY OF SPOKANE

In re the Marriage of:

SUE SNOOPIE

　　　　　　　　　　　　　　　Petitioner,

and

SAM SNOOPIE

　　　　　　　　　　　　　　　Respondent.

NO. XX-X-XXXXX-X

SUMMONS
(SM)

TO THE RESPONDENT:

1.   The petitioner has started an action in the above court requesting:

         [X]   that your marriage be dissolved.
         [ ]   a legal separation.
         [ ]   that the validity of your marriage be determined.

     Additional requests, if any, are stated in the petition, a copy of which is attached to this summons.

2.   You must respond to this summons and petition by serving a copy of your written response on the person signing this summons and by filing the original with the clerk of the court. If you do not serve your written response within 20 days (or 60 days if you are served outside of the state of Washington) after the date this summons was served on you, exclusive of the day of service, the court may enter an order of default against you, and the court may, without further notice to you, enter a decree and approve or provide for the relief requested in the petition. In the case of a dissolution of marriage, the court will not enter the final decree until at least 90 days after filing and service. If you serve a notice of appearance on the undersigned person, you are entitled to notice before an order of default or a decree may be entered.

3.   Your written response to the summons and petition must be on form WPF DR 01.0300, Response to Petition (Domestic Relations). This form may be obtained by contacting the clerk of the court at the address below, by contacting the Office of the Administrator for the Courts at (360) 705-5328, or from the Internet at the Washington State Courts homepage:

        http://www.courts.wa.gov/forms

SUMMONS (SM) - Page 1 of 2
WPF DR 01.0200 (9/2001) - CR 4.1

SELF-COUNSEL PRESS – DIV WA (2-1) 01

4.   If this action has not been filed with the court, you may demand that the petitioner file this action with the court. If you do so, the demand must be in writing and must be served upon the person signing this summons. Within 14 days after you serve the demand, the petitioner must file this action with the court, or the service on you of this summons and petition will be void.

5.   If you wish to seek the advice of an attorney in this matter, you should do so promptly so that your written response, if any, may be served on time.

6.   One method of serving a copy of your response on the petitioner is to send it by certified mail with return receipt requested.

This summons is issued pursuant to Superior Court Civil Rule 4.1 of the state of Washington.

Dated: JANUARY 10, 200-

Sue Snoopie

Signature of Lawyer or Petitioner

SUE SNOOPIE

Print or Type Name

FILE ORIGINAL OF YOUR RESPONSE
WITH THE CLERK OF THE COURT AT:

SERVE A COPY OF YOUR RESPONSE ON:

☒ Petitioner [You may list an address that is not your residential address where you agree to accept legal documents.]

[ ] Petitioner's Lawyer

SPOKANE SUPERIOR COURT
[Name of Court]

SUE SNOOPIE
[Name]

[Address]

[Address]

SAMPLE 17
RETURN OF SERVICE

SUPERIOR COURT OF WASHINGTON
COUNTY OF SPOKANE

In re the Marriage of: SUE SNOOPIE Petitioner, and SAM SNOOPIE Respondent.	NO. XX-X-XXXXX-X RETURN OF SERVICE (OPTIONAL USE) **(RTS)**

I DECLARE:

1. I am over the age of 18 years, and I am not a party to this action.

2. I served __SAM SNOOPIE__ [Name] with the following documents:

    ☒ a summons, a copy of which is attached, and a petition in this action.
    ☒ a parenting plan.
    ☒ an order to show cause.
    ☒ other: A MOTION FOR TEMPORARY RELIEF

3. The date, time and place of service were (if by mail refer to Paragraph 4 below):

    Date: __1/10/0-__   Time: __10:00__   a.m./p.m.

    Address: EAST 6000-14TH AVENUE

    YAKIMA, WA 98093

4. Service was made pursuant to Civil Rule 4(d):

    ☒ by delivery to the person named in paragraph 2 above.

[ ]   by delivery to _____ [Name], a person of suitable age and discretion residing at the respondent's usual abode.

[ ]   by publication as provided in RCW 4.28.100. (A copy of the summons is attached.)

[ ]   (check only if there is a court order authorizing service by mail) by mailing two copies postage prepaid to the person named in the order entered by the court on _____ [Date]. One copy was mailed by ordinary first class mail, the other copy was sent by certified mail return receipt requested. (Attach return receipt below.) The copies were mailed on _____ [Date].

5.   Other:

I declare under penalty of perjury under the laws of the state of Washington that the foregoing is true and correct.

Signed at _____YAKIMA, WASHINGTON_____, on ____1/10/0-_____.
                [Place]   [Date]

Percy Service
Signature

PERCY SERVICE
Print or Type Name

Fees:

Service   _____
Mileage   _____
Total   _____

(Attach Return Receipt here, if service was by mail.)

RETURN OF SERVICE (RTS) - Page 2 of 2
WPF DR 01.0250 (9/2000) - CR 4(g), RCW 4.28.080(14)   SELF-COUNSEL PRESS – DIV WA (3-2) 01

81

SUPERIOR COURT OF WASHINGTON
COUNTY OF SPOKANE

In re the Marriage of:

SUE SNOOPIE

                      Petitioner,

and

SAM SNOOPIE

                      Respondent.

NO. XX-X-XXXXX-X

MOTION AND DECLARATION FOR
DEFAULT
(MTDFL)

I. MOTION

_____SUE SNOOPIE_____ [Name] moves the court for an order of default. Venue of this action is proper as set forth in the Declaration below.

Dated: _____FEB. 2, 200-_____   _____*Sue Snoopie*_____
                                                   Signature of Lawyer or Moving Party

                                             _____SUE SNOOPIE_____
                                                     Print or Type Name

II. DECLARATION

2.1   PROPER JURISDICTION AND VENUE.

The court has proper jurisdiction and venue pursuant to the allegations of the petition at the time of filing.

The petitioner resides in ___SPOKANE COUNTY, WASHINGTON___ [County and State].

The child(ren) reside(s) in _SPOKANE COUNTY, WASHINGTON____ [County and State].

Respondent resides in ___YAKIMA COUNTY, WASHINGTON_____ [County and State].

[ ]   Other:

2.2   JURISDICTION OVER NONMOVING PARTY.

This court has jurisdiction over the nonmoving party because:

[X]   the nonmoving party is presently residing in Washington.

[ ]   the petitioner and respondent lived in Washington during their marriage and the petitioner continues to reside, or be a member of the armed forces stationed, in this state.

[ ]   the petitioner and respondent may have conceived a child while within Washington.

[ ]   Other:

2.3   SERVICE ON NONMOVING PARTY.

The nonmoving party was served with Summons, Petition, Parenting Plan [Documents] on
     1/10/200-   [Date]:

[X]   in the state of Washington.
[ ]   in _____ [State or Country where served].
       Service within the state of Washington could not be made for the following reasons:

2.4   TIME ELAPSED SINCE SERVICE ON THE NONMOVING PARTY.

[X]   The nonmoving party was served within the state of Washington and more than 20 days have elapsed since the date of service.

[ ]   The nonmoving party was served outside the state of Washington and more than 60 days have elapsed since the date of service.

[ ]   The nonmoving party was served by mail and more than 90 days have elapsed since the date of mailing.

[ ]   The nonmoving party was served by publication and more than 60 days have passed since the date of first publication.

2.5   APPEARANCE OF THE NONMOVING PARTY.

[X]   The nonmoving party has failed to appear.

[ ]   The nonmoving party has appeared, but has failed to respond.

MTN/DECL FOR DEFAULT (MTDFL) - Page 2 of 3
WPF DR 03.0100 (9/2000) - CR 55(e); RCW 26.09.030   SELF-COUNSEL PRESS – DIV WA (7-2) 01

83

SAMPLE 18—Continued

2.6   SOLDIER AND SAILORS CIVIL RELIEF ACT STATEMENT.

   [X]   The nonmoving party is not on active duty in the U.S. armed forces.
   [ ]   The nonmoving party is on active duty in the U.S. armed forces.

2.7   Other:

I declare under penalty of perjury under the laws of the state of Washington that the foregoing is true and correct.

Signed at   SPOKANE, WASHINGTON   , on   2/2/200-   .
                    [Place]   [Date]

                                        Sue Snoopie
                                        Signature

                                        SUE SNOOPIE
                                        Print or Type Name

MTN/DECL FOR DEFAULT (MTDFL) - Page 3 of 3
WPF DR 03.0100 (9/2000) - CR 55(a); RCW 26.09.030   SELF-COUNSEL PRESS – DIV WA (7-3) 01

84

SUPERIOR COURT OF WASHINGTON
COUNTY OF SPOKANE

In re the Marriage of: SUE SNOOPIE Petitioner, and SAM SNOOPIE Respondent.	NO. XX-X-XXXXX-X ORDER OF DEFAULT (ORDFL)

I. BASIS

A motion for default has been presented.

II. FINDINGS

The court FINDS that:

2.1   PROPER JURISDICTION AND VENUE.

The court has proper jurisdiction and venue.

2.2   SERVICE ON NONMOVING PARTY.

The nonmoving party was served with   SUMMONS, PETITION, AND PROPOSED
 PARENTING PLAN
on   JANUARY 10, 200-   [Date].

2.3   TIME ELAPSED SINCE SERVICE.

[X]   The nonmoving party was served within the state of Washington and more than 20 days have
elapsed since the date of service.

[ ]   The nonmoving party was served outside the state of Washington and more than 60 days have
elapsed since the date of service.

ORD OF DEFAULT (DISSO)(ORDFL) - Page 1 of 2
WPF DR 03.0200 (9/2000) - CR 55(a); RCW 26.09.020   SELF-COUNSEL PRESS – DIV WA (8-1) 01

85

[ ]   The nonmoving party was served by mail and more than 90 days have elapsed since the date of mailing.

[ ]   The nonmoving party was served by publication and more than 60 days have passed since the date of first publication.

2.4   APPEARANCE.

☒   The nonmoving party has failed to appear.

[ ]   The nonmoving party has appeared but has failed to respond.

2.5   OTHER.

III. ORDER

IT IS ORDERED that the nonmoving party is in default.

Dated: __2/2/200-_____   _J.M. Commissioner_____
                                                  JUDGE/COMMISSIONER

Presented by:

_Sue Snoopie_____
Signature

__SUE SNOOPIE_____
Print or Type Name

SUPERIOR COURT OF WASHINGTON
COUNTY OF SPOKANE

In re the Marriage of:

SUE SNOOPIE

Petitioner,

and

SAM SNOOPIE

Respondent.

NO. XX-X-XXXXX-X

RESPONSE TO PETITION
(DOMESTIC RELATIONS)
(RSP)

TO THE ABOVE-NAMED PETITIONER:

I. RESPONSE

1.1 ADMISSIONS AND DENIALS.

The allegations of the petition in this matter are ADMITTED or DENIED as follows (check only one for each paragraph):

<u>Paragraph of the Petition</u>

1.1	[X]	Admitted	[ ]	Denied	[ ]	Lacks Information
1.2	[X]	Admitted	[ ]	Denied	[ ]	Lacks Information
1.3	[X]	Admitted	[ ]	Denied	[ ]	Lacks Information
1.4	[X]	Admitted	[ ]	Denied	[ ]	Lacks Information
1.5	[X]	Admitted	[ ]	Denied	[ ]	Lacks Information
1.6	[X]	Admitted	[ ]	Denied	[ ]	Lacks Information
1.7	[ ]	Admitted	[X]	Denied	[ ]	Lacks Information
1.8	[X]	Admitted	[ ]	Denied	[ ]	Lacks Information

RESPONSE TO PETITION (RSP) - Page 1 of 3
WPF DR 01.0300 (9/2001) - RCW 26.09.0300

1.9	[X]	Admitted	[ ]	Denied	[ ]	Lacks Information
1.10	[ ]	Admitted	[X]	Denied	[ ]	Lacks Information
1.11	[X]	Admitted	[ ]	Denied	[ ]	Lacks Information
1.12	[X]	Admitted	[ ]	Denied	[ ]	Lacks Information
1.13	[ ]	Admitted	[X]	Denied	[ ]	Lacks Information
1.14	[X]	Admitted	[ ]	Denied	[ ]	Lacks Information
1.15	[X]	Admitted	[ ]	Denied	[ ]	Lacks Information

The allegations of the petition which are denied, are denied for the following reasons:

This is not a required pleading.

1.2   NOTICE OF FURTHER PROCEEDINGS.

Notice of all further proceedings in this matter should be sent to the address below.

1.3   OTHER.

RESPONSE TO PETITION (RSP) - Page 2 of 3
WPF DR 01.0300 (9/2001) - RCW 26.09.0300

II. REQUEST FOR RELIEF.

[ ]   Does not apply.

☒   The respondent requests the court to grant the relief requested below.

        ☒   Enter a decree.

        [ ]   Provide reasonable maintenance for the [ ] husband [ ] wife.

        [ ]   Approve my parenting plan for the dependent children.

        [ ]   Determine support for the dependent children pursuant to the Washington State Support Schedule.

        [ ]   Approve the separation agreement.

        ☒   Dispose of property and liabilities.

        [ ]   Change name of wife to: _____.

        [ ]   Change name of husband to: _____.

        [ ]   Enter a continuing restraining order.

        [ ]   Order payment of day care expenses for the children.

        ☒   Award the tax exemptions for the dependent children as follows:

            TO THE HUSBAND.

        [ ]   Order payment of attorney's fees, other professional fees and costs.

        [ ]   Other:

Dated: __02/01/200-_____   *Sam Snoopie*_____

                                          Signature of Lawyer or Respondent

                                          SAM SNOOPIE_____

                                          Print or Type Name

                                          Notice to party: You may list an address that is not your residential address where you agree to accept legal documents.

                                          111 SECOND STREET_____

                                          [Address]

                                          YAKIMA, WA 98190_____

RESPONSE TO PETITION (RSP) - Page 3 of 3
WPF DR 01.0300 (9/2001) - RCW 26.09.0300

SAMPLE 21
TEMPORARY ORDER

SUPERIOR COURT OF WASHINGTON
COUNTY OF SPOKANE

In re the Marriage of:

SUE SNOOPIE

Petitioner,

and

SAM SNOOPIE

Respondent.

NO. XX-X-XXXXX-X

TEMPORARY ORDER
(TMO)

☒ Clerk's Action Required

I. JUDGMENT/ORDER SUMMARIES

1.1 RESTRAINING ORDER SUMMARY:
☒ Does not apply.   [ ] Restraining Order Summary is set forth below:

Name of person(s) restrained: _____. Name of person(s)
Name of person(s) protected: _____. **See paragraph 3.1**.

VIOLATION OF A RESTRAINING ORDER IN PARAGRAPH 3.1 WITH ACTUAL NOTICE OF ITS TERMS IS A CRIMINAL OFFENSE UNDER CHAPTER 26.50 RCW AND WILL SUBJECT THE VIOLATOR TO ARREST. RCW 26.09.060.

1.2 MONEY JUDGMENT SUMMARY:

[ ]   Does not apply.
[ ]   Judgment Summary is set forth below.

A.   Judgment creditor   _____
B.   Judgment debtor   _____
C.   Principal judgment amount $ _____
D.   Interest to date of judgment $ _____
E.   Attorney's fees $ _____
F.   Costs $ _____
G.   Other recovery amount $ _____
H.   Principal judgment shall bear interest at _____% per annum
I.   Attorney's fees, costs and other recovery amounts shall bear interest at _____% per annum

90

J.   Attorney for judgment creditor   _____

K.   Attorney for judgment debtor   _____

L.   Other:

II. BASIS

A motion for a temporary order was presented to this court and the court finds reasonable cause to issue the order.

III. ORDER

It is ORDERED that:

3.1   RESTRAINING ORDER:

VIOLATION OF A RESTRAINING ORDER IN PARAGRAPH 3.1 WITH ACTUAL NOTICE OF ITS TERMS IS A CRIMINAL OFFENSE UNDER CHAPTER 26.50 RCW AND WILL SUBJECT THE VIOLATOR TO ARREST. RCW 26.09.060

[ ]   Does not apply.

[ ]   The [ ] husband [ ] wife is restrained and enjoined from molesting or disturbing the peace of the other party or of any child.

[ ]   The [ ] husband [ ] wife is restrained and enjoined from going onto the grounds of or entering the home, work place or school of the other party, or the day care or school of the following named children: _____

[ ]   The [ ] husband [ ] wife is restrained and enjoined from knowingly coming within or knowingly remaining within _____ (distance) of the home, work place or school of the other party, or the day care or school of these children: _____

CLERK'S ACTION/LAW ENFORCEMENT ACTION:

[ ]   This order shall be filed forthwith in the clerk's office and entered of record. The clerk of the court shall forward a copy of this order on or before the next judicial day to _____ (name of appropriate law enforcement agency) which shall forthwith enter this order into any computer-based criminal intelligence system available in this state used by law enforcement agencies to list outstanding warrants. **(A law enforcement information sheet must be completed by the party or the party's attorney and provided with this order before this order will be entered into the law enforcement computer system.)**

EXPIRATION DATE:

This restraining order will expire in 12 months and shall be removed from any computer-based criminal intelligence system available in this state used by law enforcement agencies to list outstanding warrants, unless a new order is issued, or unless the court sets forth another expiration date here: _____ (month/day/year).

3.2   TEMPORARY RELIEF.

[ ]   The [ ] husband [ ] wife shall pay the other party $_____ per month maintenance.

Starting Date: _____
Day(s) of the month payment is due: _____

Payments shall be made to:

[ ]   the Washington State Child Support Registry (if child support is ordered).
[ ]   directly to the other spouse.
[ ]   the clerk of this court as trustee for remittance to the other spouse (if there are no dependent children).
[ ]   Other:

[X]   Child support shall be paid in accordance with the order of child support, signed by the court.

[X]   The parties shall comply with the Temporary Parenting Plan signed by the court.

[X]   The [X] husband [ ] wife is restrained and enjoined from transferring, removing, encumbering, concealing or in any way disposing of any property except in the usual course of business or for the necessities of life and requiring each party to notify the other of any extraordinary expenditures made after the order is issued.

[X]   The [ ] husband [ ] wife is restrained and enjoined from removing any of the children from the state of Washington.

[X]   The [X] husband [ ] wife is restrained and enjoined from assigning, transferring, borrowing, lapsing, surrendering or changing entitlement of any insurance policies of either or both parties whether medical, health, life or auto insurance.

[ ]   The [ ] husband [ ] wife shall surrender any deadly weapon in his or her immediate possession or control or subject to his or her immediate possession or control to: ....
_____ (Name or agency).

[X]   Each party shall be immediately responsible for their own future debts whether incurred by credit card or loan, security interest or mortgage.

[ ]   Responsibility for the debts of the parties is divided as follows:

[X]   The family home shall be occupied by the [ ] husband [X] wife.

[ ]   Use of property shall be as follows:

TEMP ORDER (TMO) - Page 3 of 4
WPF DR 04.0250 (9/2001) - RCW 26.09.060; .110; .120; .194   SELF-COUNSEL PRESS – DIV WA (10-3) 01

92

SAMPLE 21—Continued

[ ]   The [ ] husband [ ] wife shall vacate the family home. You have a right to keep your residential address confidential. [ ] _____ [Name] waives confidentiality of the address which is: _____

[ ]   The [ ] husband [ ] wife shall pay temporary attorney's fees, other professional fees and costs in the amount of $_____ to:

[ ]   Other:

3.3   BOND OR SECURITY.

    [X]   Does not apply.
    [ ]   The filing of a bond or the posting of security is waived.
    [ ]   Other:

3.4   OTHER:

Dated: __2/2/200-_____   _J.M. Commissioner_____
                           JUDGE/COMMISSIONER

Presented by: Approved for entry:
                                    Notice of presentation waived:

_Sue Snoopie_____   _____
Signature   Signature

SUE SNOOPIE_____   _____
Print or Type Name   Print or Type Name

TEMP ORDER (TMO) - Page 4 of 4
WPF DR 04.0250 (9/2001) - RCW 26.09.060; .110; .120; .194   SELF-COUNSEL PRESS – DIV WA (10-4) 01

93

SUPERIOR COURT OF WASHINGTON
COUNTY OF SPOKANE

In re the Marriage of:

SUE SNOOPIE

Petitioner,

and

SAM SNOOPIE

Respondent.

NO. XX-X-XXXXX-X

MOTION AND DECLARATION FOR
TEMPORARY ORDER
(MTAF)

I. MOTION

Based on the declaration below, the undersigned moves the court for a temporary order which:

[ ] orders temporary maintenance.

[X] orders child support as determined pursuant to the Washington State Support Schedule.

[X] approves the parenting plan which is proposed by the [ ] husband [ ] wife.

[X] restrains or enjoins the [X] husband [ ] wife from transferring, removing, encumbering, concealing or in any way disposing of any property except in the usual course of business or for the necessities of life and requiring each party to notify the other of any extraordinary expenditures made after the order is issued.

[ ] restrains or enjoins the [ ] husband [ ] wife from molesting or disturbing the peace of the other party or of any child.

[X] restrains or enjoins the [X] husband [ ] wife from going onto the grounds of or entering the home, work place or school of the other party or the day care or school of the following named children:
SUSIE SNOOPIE   .

[ ] restrains or enjoins the [ ] husband [ ] wife from knowingly coming within or knowingly remaining within _____ (distance) of the home, work place or school of the other party or the day care or school of the following children:_____
_____.

[X] restrains or enjoins the [X] husband [ ] wife from removing any of the children from the state of Washington.

[X] restrains or enjoins the [X] husband [ ] wife from assigning, transferring, borrowing, lapsing, surrendering or changing entitlement of any insurance policies of either or both parties whether medical, health, life or auto insurance.

[ ] **(IF THIS BOX IS CHECKED CLEAR AND CONVINCING REASONS FOR THIS REQUEST MUST BE PRESENTED IN THE DECLARATION BELOW.)** requires the
[ ] husband [ ] wife to surrender any deadly weapon in his or her immediate possession or control or subject to his or her immediate possession or control to the sheriff of the county having jurisdiction of this proceeding, to his or her lawyer or to a person designated by the court.

[X]   makes each party immediately responsible for their own future debts whether incurred by credit card or loan, security interest or mortgage.

[ ]   divides responsibility for the debts of the parties.

[X]   authorizes the family home to be occupied by the [ ] husband [X] wife.

[ ]   orders the use of property.

[ ]   requires the [ ] husband [ ] wife to vacate the family home.

[ ]   requires the [ ] husband [ ] wife to pay temporary attorney's fees, other professional fees and costs in the amount of $_____ to:

[ ]   appoints a guardian ad litem on behalf of the minor children.

[ ]   other:

Dated: 01/10/200-   *Sue Snoopie*

                                              Signature of Lawyer or Moving Party

                                          SUE SNOOPIE

                                          Print or Type Name

II. DECLARATION

Temporary relief is required because:

The respondent and I have a minor child who is dependent on us. Our child resides with me. It is in the best interest of our child to continue residing with me. (See Declaration in Support of Parenting Plan and Financial Declaration, which are filed with this motion.) I need to have the family home as a residence for the child and myself. I have no other place to go. The respondent is currently residing out of the home. I feel that I need to be protected fromt he respondent's incurring debt and selling property as he has done so in the past.

If the surrender of deadly weapons is requested, list reasons:

I declare under penalty of perjury under the laws of the state of Washington that the foregoing is true and correct.

Signed at   SPOKANE, WASHINGTON   on   01/10/200-   .

                  [City and State]   [Date]

                                          Sue Snoopie

                                          Signature

                                          SUE SNOOPIE

                                          Print or Type Name

DO NOT ATTACH FINANCIAL RECORDS TO THIS DECLARATION. FINANCIAL RECORDS SHOULD BE SERVED ON THE OTHER PARTY AND FILED WITH THE COURT SEPARATELY USING THE SEALED FINANCIAL SOURCE DOCUMENTS COVER SHEET (WPF DRPSCU 09.0220). IF FILED SEPARATELY USING THE COVER SHEET, THE RECORDS WILL BE SEALED TO PROTECT YOUR PRIVACY

MTN/DECL FOR TEMP ORD (MTAF) - Page 2 of 2
WPF DR 04.0100 (9/2001) - RCW 26.09.060, .110, .120, .194   SELF-COUNSEL PRESS -- DIV WA (23-2) 01

95

FINANCIAL DECLARATION

SUPERIOR COURT OF WASHINGTON
COUNTY OF SPOKANE

In re:

SUE SNOOPIE

                            Petitioner.

and

SAM SNOOPIE

                            Respondent.

NO. XX-X-XXXXX-X

FINANCIAL DECLARATION
[ ] PETITIONER
[X] RESPONDENT
(FNDCLR)

Name: SAM SNOOPIE   Date of Birth: 5/2/69

I. SUMMARY OF BASIC INFORMATION

Declarant's Total Monthly Net Income (from § 3.3 below) $ 1,369.20

Declarant's Total Monthly Household Expenses (from § 5.9 below) $ _____

Declarant's Total Monthly Debt Expenses (from § 5.11 below) $ _____

Declarant's Total Monthly Expenses (from § 5.12 below) $ _____

Estimate of the other party's gross monthly income (from § 3.1f below)   [ ] $ _____

                                            [ ] unknown

II. PERSONAL INFORMATION

2.1   Occupation: DRIVER LOADER
2.2   The highest year of education completed: 12th
2.3   Are you presently employed? [X] Yes [ ] No
     a. If yes: (1)   Where do you work. Employer's name and address must be listed on the Confidential Information Form.

                  (2)   When did you start work there (month/year)?   AUGUST 1997

     b. If no: (1)   When did you last work (month/year)? _____
                  (2)   What were your gross monthly earnings? $ _____
                  (3)   Why are you presently unemployed?

III. INCOME INFORMATION

If child support is at issue, complete the Washington State Child Support Worksheet(s), skip Paragraphs 3.1 and 3.2. If maintenance, fees, costs or debts are at issue and child support is NOT an issue this entire section should be completed. (Estimate of other party's income information is optional.)

3.1   GROSS MONTHLY INCOME.
       If you are paid on a weekly basis, multiply your weekly gross pay by 4.3 to determine your monthly wages and salaries. If you are paid every two weeks, multiply your gross pay by 2.15. If you are paid twice monthly, multiply your gross pay by 2. If you are paid once a month, list that amount below.

		Petitioner	Respondent
a.	Wages and Salaries	$	$ 1,646.67
b.	Interest and Dividend Income	$	$
c.	Business Income	$	$
d.	Spousal Maintenance From Other Relationships	$	$
e.	Other Income	$	$
f.	Total Gross Monthly Income (add lines 3.1a through 3.1e)	$	$ 1,646.67
g.	Actual Gross Income (Year-to-date)	$	$

3.2   MONTHLY DEDUCTIONS FROM GROSS INCOME.

		Petitioner	Respondent
a.	Income Taxes	$	$ 161.00
b.	FICA/Self-employment Taxes	$	$ 125.97
c.	State Industrial Insurance Deductions	$	$
d.	MANDATORY Union/Professional Dues	$	$
e.	Pension Plan Payments	$	$
f.	Spousal Maintenance Paid	$	$
g.	Normal Business Expenses	$	$
h.	Total Deductions from Gross Income (add lines 3.2a through 3.2g)	$	$ 286.97

3.3   MONTHLY NET INCOME. (Line 3.1f minus line 3.2h or $ _____ $ 1,359.70
       line 3 from the Child Support Worksheet(s).)

3.4   MISCELLANEOUS INCOME.

		Petitioner	Respondent
a.	Child support received from other relationships	$	$
b.	Other miscellaneous income (list source and amounts)		
	_____	$	$
	_____	$	$
	_____	$	$
	_____	$	$
c.	Total Miscellaneous Income (add lines 3.4a through 3.4b)	$	$ -0-

3.5   Income of Other Adults in Household $ _____ $ _____

3.6   If the income of either party is disputed, state monthly income you believe is correct and explain below:

SAMPLE 23—Continued

IV. AVAILABLE ASSETS

4.1	Cash on hand	$ min
4.2	On deposit in banks	$ -0-
4.3	Stocks and bonds, cash value of life insurance	$ -0-
4.4	Other liquid assets:	$

V. MONTHLY EXPENSE INFORMATION

Monthly expenses for myself and _____ dependents are: (Expenses should be calculated for the future, after separation, based on the anticipated residential schedule for the children.)

5.1 HOUSING.

Rent, 1st mortgage or contract payments	$ 200.00
Installment payments for other mortgages or encumbrances	$
Taxes & insurance (if not in monthly payment)	$
Total Housing	$ 200.00

5.2 UTILITIES.

Heat (gas & oil)	$
Electricity	$
Water, sewer, garbage	$
Telephone	$
Cable	$
Other	$
Total Utilities	$ -0-

5.3 FOOD AND SUPPLIES.

Food for _____ persons	$
Supplies (paper, tobacco, pets)	$
Meals eaten out	$ 100.00
Other	$
Total Food Supplies	$ 100.00

5.4 CHILDREN.

Day Care/Babysitting	$
Clothing	$
Tuition (if any)	$
Other child related expenses	$
Total Expenses Children	$

5.5 TRANSPORTATION.

Vehicle payments or leases	$ 440.00
Vehicle insurance & license	$ 182.00
Vehicle gas, oil, ordinary maintenance	$ 200.00
Parking	$
Other transportation expenses	$
Total Transportation	$ 822.00

FINANCIAL DECLARATION (FNDCLR) - Page 3 of 5
WPF DR 01.0550 (9/2001) - RCW 26.18.220 (1)

SELF-COUNSEL PRESS – DIV WA (6-3) 01

98

5.6   HEALTH CARE. (Omit if fully covered)

Insurance $ 59.00
Uninsured dental, orthodontic, medical, eye care expenses $ 10.00
Other uninsured health expenses $
Total Health Care $ 69.00

5.7   PERSONAL EXPENSES (Not including children).

Clothing $
Hair care/personal care expenses $
Clubs and recreation $
Education $
Books, newspapers, magazines, photos $
Gifts $
Other $ 5.00
Total Personal Expenses $ 5.00

5.8   MISCELLANEOUS EXPENSES.

Life insurance (if not deducted from income) $
Other _____ $
Other _____ $
Total Miscellaneous Expenses $

5.9   TOTAL HOUSEHOLD EXPENSES (The total of Paragraphs 5.1 through 5.8) $ 1,196.00

5.10   INSTALLMENT DEBTS INCLUDED IN PARAGRAPHS 5.1 THROUGH 5.8.

Creditor	Description of Debt	Balance	Month of Last Payment
1st Ubterstate	car loan	11,000	November, 200-

5.11   OTHER DEBTS AND MONTHLY EXPENSES NOT INCLUDED IN PARAGRAPHS 5.1 THROUGH 5.8.

Creditor	Description of Debt	Balance	Month of Last Payment	Amount of Monthly Payment
1st Ubterstate	car loan	11,000	Nov. 200-	$ 440.00
Cascade Valley Hospital	hernia operation, etc	1,400	none	$ all due
				$
				$
				$
				$
				$

Total Monthly Payments for Other Debts and Monthly Expenses $

FINANCIAL DECLARATION (FNDCLR) - Page 4 of 5
WPF DR 01.0550 (9/2001) - RCW 26.18.220 (1)   SELF-COUNSEL PRESS – DIV WA (8-4) 01

5.12   TOTAL EXPENSES (Add Paragraphs 5.9 and 5.11) $ _____

VI. ATTORNEY FEES

6.1   Amount paid for attorney fees and costs to date: $ _____
6.2   The source of this money was:
6.3   Fees and costs incurred to date: $ _____
6.4   Arrangements for attorney fees and costs are:

6.5   Other:

I declare under penalty of perjury under the laws of the state of Washington that the foregoing is true and correct.

Signed at ___ARLINGTON, WA_____   on ___NOVEMBER 23, 200-____ .
                    [Place]   [Date]

_____*Sam Snoopie*_____
Signature

___SAM SNOOPIE_____
Print or Type Name

The following financial records are being provided to the other party and filed separately with the court:

Financial records pertaining to myself:

[X] Individual [ ] Partnership or Corporate Income Tax returns for the years __200-, 200-__
_____   including all W-2s and schedules:

[X] Pay stubs for the dates of __JUNE TO NOVEMBER, 200-_____
_____

[ ] Other:_____
_____
_____
_____
_____
_____
_____

DO NOT ATTACH THESE FINANCIAL RECORDS TO THE FINANCIAL DECLARATION. THESE FINANCIAL RECORDS SHOULD BE SERVED ON THE OTHER PARTY AND FILED WITH THE COURT SEPARATELY USING THE SEALED FINANCIAL SOURCE DOCUMENTS COVER SHEET (WPF DRPSCU 09.0220). IF FILED SEPARATELY USING THE COVER SHEET, THE RECORDS WILL BE SEALED TO PROTECT YOUR PRIVACY (ALTHOUGH THEY WILL BE AVAILABLE TO THE OTHER PARTIES IN THE CASE, THEIR ATTORNEYS, AND CERTAIN OTHER INTERESTED PERSONS. SEE GR 22 (C)(2)).

FINANCIAL DECLARATION (FNDCLR) - Page 5 of 5
WPF DR 01.0550 (9/2001) - RCW 26.18.220 (1)   SELF-COUNSEL PRESS – DIV WA (6-5) 01

100

SAMPLE 24
DECLARATION IN SUPPORT OF PARENTING PLAN

SUPERIOR COURT OF WASHINGTON
COUNTY OF   SPOKANE

In re:

SUE SNOOPIE

                                              Petitioner,

and

SAM SNOOPIE

                                              Respondent.

NO.   XX-X-XXXXX-X

DECLARATION IN SUPPORT
OF PARENTING PLAN
(DCLR)

(COMPLETE A SEPARATE FORM FOR EACH CHILD IF NECESSARY)

This declaration is made by the [ ] father [X] mother.

1.   _____SUSIE SNOOPIE_____ [name of child(ren)] has/have resided with the following person(s) during the past 12 months:

Name	Length of Time Child Resided With This Person
SUE AND SAM SNOOPIE	ALL HER LIFE

2.   (a)   The mother's performance of parenting functions relating to the daily needs of the child(ren) during the past 12 months:
            Mother has performed all parenting functions for the child for the past six months, and prior to that, provided at least 50 percent of the parenting functions.

      (b)   The mother's work schedule for the past 12 months:
            The mother works 9 to 5, Monday through Friday.

(c)   The mother's current work schedule:

9 to 5, Monday through Friday.

3.   (a)   The father's performance of parenting functions relating to the daily needs of the child(ren) during the past 12 months:

None during the past six months. Less than 50 percent prior to that time.

(b)   The father's work schedule for the past 12 months:

Unknown.

(c)   The father's current work schedule:

Unknown.

4.   (a)   The child-care schedule for the past 12 months:

Child has been in day care from 8:30 a.m. to 5:30 p.m. Monday through Friday for the past twelve months.

(b)   The current child-care schedule:

Same as above.

5.   Any circumstances under RCW 26.09.191 that are likely to pose a serious risk to the child(ren) and that warrant limitation on the award to a parent of temporary residence or time with the child(ren) pending entry of a permanent parenting plan are set forth in Part II of my proposed temporary parenting plan.

6.   OTHER:

I declare under penalty of perjury under the laws of the state of Washington that the foregoing is true and correct.

Signed at ___SPOKANE, WASHINGTON___ [Place] on ___2/2/200-___ [Date].

_Sue Snoopie_____
Signature

SUE SNOOPIE_____
Print or Type Name

SUPERIOR COURT OF WASHINGTON
COUNTY OF SPOKANE

In re the Marriage of: SUE SNOOPIE Petitioner, and SAM SNOOPIE Respondent.	NO. XX-X-XXXXX-X ORDER OF CHILD SUPPORT (ORS) **Clerk's Action Required**

I. JUDGMENT SUMMARY

[ ]   Does not apply because no attorney's fees or back child support has been ordered.
[ ]   The judgment summary:

A.   Judgment creditor   _____
B.   Judgment debtor   _____
C.   Principal judgment amount (back child support) $ _____
      from _____ [Date] to _____ [Date]
D.   Interest to date of Judgment $ _____
E.   Attorney's fees $ _____
F.   Costs $ _____
G.   Other recovery amount $ _____
H.   Principal judgment shall bear interest at _____ % per annum
I.   Attorney's fees, costs and other recovery amounts shall bear interest at _____ % per annum
J.   Attorney for judgment creditor   _____
K.   Attorney for judgment debtor   _____
L.   Other:

II. BASIS

2.1   TYPE OF PROCEEDING.

       This order is entered pursuant to:
       [ ]   a decree of dissolution, legal separation or a declaration of invalidity.

ORDER OF CHILD SUPPORT (ORS) - Page 1 of 10
WPF DR 01.0500 (9/2001) - RCW 26.09.175; 26.26.132(5)   SELF-COUNSEL PRESS – DIV WA (22-1) 01

103

[ ]   an order determining parentage.
[ ]   an order for modification of child support.
[ ]   a hearing for temporary child support.
[ ]   an order of adjustment.
[ ]   an order for modification of a custody decree or parenting plan.
[ ]   Other:

2.2   CHILD SUPPORT WORKSHEET.

The child support worksheet which has been approved by the court is attached to this order and is incorporated by reference or has been initialed and filed separately and is incorporated by reference.

2.3   OTHER:

III. FINDINGS AND ORDER

IT IS ORDERED that:

3.1   CHILDREN FOR WHOM SUPPORT IS REQUIRED.

Name (first/last)   Age

SUSIE SNOOPIE

3.2   PERSON PAYING SUPPORT (OBLIGOR).

Name (first/last): SAM SNOOPIE
Birth date: 5/2/69
Service Address: [You may list an address that is not your residential address where you agree to accept legal documents.] 6000-14TH AVENUE, SPOKANE, WA 98093

THE OBLIGOR PARENT MUST IMMEDIATELY FILE WITH THE COURT AND THE WASHINGTON STATE CHILD SUPPORT REGISTRY, AND UPDATE AS NECESSARY, THE CONFIDENTIAL INFORMATION FORM REQUIRED BY RCW 26.23.050.

THE OBLIGOR PARENT SHALL UPDATE THE INFORMATION REQUIRED BY PARAGRAPH 3.2 PROMPTLY AFTER ANY CHANGE IN THE INFORMATION. THE DUTY TO UPDATE THE INFORMATION CONTINUES AS LONG AS ANY MONTHLY SUPPORT REMAINS DUE OR ANY UNPAID SUPPORT DEBT REMAINS DUE UNDER THIS ORDER.

ORDER OF CHILD SUPPORT (ORS) - Page 2 of 10
WPF DR 01.0500 (9/2001) - RCW 26.09.175; 26.26.132(5)   SELF-COUNSEL PRESS – DIV WA (22-2) 01

104

     [X]   Monthly Net Income: $ 1,000

[ ]   The income of the obligor is imputed at $ _____ because:

      [ ]   the obligor's income is unknown.
      [ ]   the obligor is voluntarily unemployed.
      [ ]   the obligor is voluntarily underemployed.
      [ ]   other:

3.3   PERSON RECEIVING SUPPORT (OBLIGEE):

Name (first/last): SUE SNOOPIE
Birth date: 4/2/70
Service Address: [You may list an address that is not your residential address where you agree to accept legal documents.]

    123 BEAGLE STREET, SPOKANE, WA 99201

THE OBLIGEE PARENT MUST IMMEDIATELY FILE WITH THE COURT AND THE WASHINGTON STATE CHILD SUPPORT REGISTRY AND UPDATE AS NECESSARY THE CONFIDENTIAL INFORMATION FORM REQUIRED BY RCW 26.23.050.

THE OBLIGEE PARENT SHALL UPDATE THE INFORMATION REQUIRED BY PARAGRAPH 3.3 PROMPTLY AFTER ANY CHANGE IN THE INFORMATION. THE DUTY TO UPDATE THE INFORMATION CONTINUES AS LONG AS ANY MONTHLY SUPPORT REMAINS DUE OR ANY UNPAID SUPPORT DEBT REMAINS DUE UNDER THIS ORDER.

    [X]   Monthly Net Income: $ 1,000.00
    [ ]   The income of the obligee is imputed at $ _____ because:

      [ ]   the obligee's income is unknown.
      [ ]   the obligee is voluntarily unemployed.
      [ ]   the obligee is voluntarily underemployed.
      [ ]   other:

The obligor may be able to seek reimbursement for day care or special child rearing expenses not actually incurred. RCW 26.19.080.

3.4   SERVICE OF PROCESS.

SERVICE OF PROCESS ON THE OBLIGOR AT THE ADDRESS REQUIRED BY PARAGRAPH 3.2 OR ANY UPDATED ADDRESS, OR ON THE OBLIGEE AT THE ADDRESS REQUIRED BY PARAGRAPH 3.3 OR ANY UPDATED ADDRESS, MAY BE ALLOWED OR ACCEPTED AS ADEQUATE IN ANY PROCEEDING TO ESTABLISH, ENFORCE OR MODIFY A CHILD SUPPORT ORDER BETWEEN THE PARTIES BY DELIVERY OF WRITTEN NOTICE TO THE OBLIGOR OR OBLIGEE AT THE LAST ADDRESS PROVIDED.

3.5   TRANSFER PAYMENT.

    [ ]   The obligor parent shall pay $ _____ per month.

ORDER OF CHILD SUPPORT (ORS) - Page 3 of 10
WPF DR 01.0500 (9/2001) - RCW 26.09.175; 26.26.132(5)   SELF-COUNSEL PRESS – DIV WA (22-3) 01

105

[ ]   The obligor parent shall pay the following amounts per month for the following children:

Name	Amount
_____	$_____
_____	$_____
_____	$_____
_____	$_____
TOTAL MONTHLY AMOUNT	$_____

[ ]   The parents' combined monthly net income exceeds $7,000 and the court sets child support in excess of the advisory amount because:

[ ]   If one of the children changes age brackets or terminates support, child support shall be as follows:

[ ]   Other:

THE OBLIGOR PARENT'S PRIVILEGES TO OBTAIN OR MAINTAIN A LICENSE, CERTIFICATE, REGISTRATION, PERMIT, APPROVAL, OR OTHER SIMILAR DOCUMENT ISSUED BY A LICENSING ENTITY EVIDENCING ADMISSION TO OR GRANTING AUTHORITY TO ENGAGE IN A PROFESSION, OCCUPATION, BUSINESS, INDUSTRY, RECREATIONAL PURSUIT, OR THE OPERATION OF A MOTOR VEHICLE MAY BE DENIED OR MAY BE SUSPENDED IF THE OBLIGOR PARENT IS NOT IN COMPLIANCE WITH THIS SUPPORT ORDER AS PROVIDED IN CHAPTER 74.20A REVISED CODE OF WASHINGTON.

3.6   STANDARD CALCULATION.

$ _____213_____ per month. (See Worksheet line 15.)

3.7   REASONS FOR DEVIATION FROM STANDARD CALCULATION.

[X] The child support amount ordered in paragraph 3.5 does not deviate from the standard calculation.
[ ] The child support amount ordered in paragraph 3.5 deviates from the standard calculation for the following reasons:

        [ ] Income of a new spouse of the parent requesting a deviation for other reasons;
        [ ] Income of other adults in the household of the parent requesting a deviation for other reasons;
        [ ] Child support actually paid or received for other children from other relationships;
        [ ] Gifts;
        [ ] Prizes;
        [ ] Possession of wealth;
        [ ] Extraordinary income of a child;
        [ ] Tax planning which results in greater benefit to the children;
        [ ] A nonrecurring source of income;
        [ ] Extraordinary debt not voluntarily incurred;

ORDER OF CHILD SUPPORT (ORS) - Page 4 of 10
WPF DR 01.0500 (9/2001) - RCW 26.09.175; 26.26.132(5)   SELF-COUNSEL PRESS – DIV WA (22-4) 01

106

[ ] A significant disparity in the living costs of the parents due to conditions beyond their control;

[ ] Special needs of disabled children;

[ ] Special medical, educational, or psychological needs of the children;

[ ] The child spends a significant amount of time with the parent who is obligated to make a support transfer payment. The deviation does not result in insufficient funds in the receiving parent's household to meet the basic needs of the child. The child does not receive public assistance;

[ ] Children from other relationships;

[ ] Costs incurred or anticipated to be incurred by the parents in compliance with court-ordered reunification efforts or under a voluntary placement agreement with an agency supervising the child;

[ ] Other:

The factual basis for these reasons is as follows:

[ ] Other:

3.8   REASONS WHY REQUEST FOR DEVIATION WAS DENIED.

[X]   Does not apply. A deviation was ordered.

[ ]   A deviation was not requested.

[ ]   The deviation sought by the [ ] obligor [ ] obligee was denied because:

    [ ]   no good reason exists to justify deviation.

    [ ]   Other:

3.9   STARTING DATE AND DAY TO BE PAID.

Starting Date: 5/1/200-

Day(s) of the month support is due: _____

3.10   INCREMENTAL PAYMENTS.

[X]   Does not apply.

[ ]   This is a modification of child support. Pursuant to RCW 26.09.170 (8)(a) and (c), the obligation has been modified by more than 30 percent and the change would cause significant hardship. The increase in the child support obligation set forth in Paragraph 3.5 shall be implemented in two equal increments, one at the time of this order and the second on _____ [Date] six months from the entry of this order.

ORDER OF CHILD SUPPORT (ORS) - Page 5 of 10
WPF DR 01.0500 (9/2001) - RCW 26.09.175; 26.26.132(5)   SELF-COUNSEL PRESS – DIV WA (22-5) 01

107

3.11   HOW SUPPORT PAYMENTS SHALL BE MADE.

Select *either* Enforcement and Collection *or* Payment Processing Only:

[X]   Enforcement and collection: The Division of Child Support provides support enforcement services for this case (this includes public assistance cases, cases in which a parent has requested services from DCS, and cases in which a parent signs the application for services from DCS on the bottom of the support order). Support payments shall be made to:

> Washington State Support Registry
> P. O. Box 45868
> Olympia, WA 98504
> Phone: 1-800-922-4306 or
>   1-800-442-5437

[ ]   Payment processing only: The Division of Child Support does not provide support enforcement services for this case. Support payments shall be made to:

[ ]   _____

       _____

[ ]   Washington State Support Registry
       P. O. Box 45868
       Olympia, WA 98504
       Phone: 1-800-922-4306 or
                     1-800-442-5437
       (DCS will process payments but will not take any collection action.)

A party required to make payments to the Washington State Support Registry will not receive credit for a payment made to any other party or entity. The obligor parent shall keep the registry informed whether he or she has access to health insurance coverage at reasonable cost and, if so, to provide the health insurance policy information.

3.12   WAGE WITHHOLDING ACTION.

Withholding action may be taken against wages, earnings, assets, or benefits, and liens enforced against real and personal property under the child support statutes of this or any other state, without further notice to the obligor parent at any time after entry of this order unless an alternative provision is made below:

[If the court orders immediate wage withholding in a case where Division of Child Support does not provide support enforcement services, a mandatory wage assignment under Chap. 26.18 RCW must be entered and support payments must be made to the Support Registry.]

[X]   Wage withholding, by notice of payroll deduction or other income withholding action under Chapter 26.18 RCW or Chapter 74.20A RCW, without further notice to the obligor, is delayed until a payment is past due, because:
    [ ]   the parties have reached a written agreement that the court approves that provides for an alternate arrangement.
    [ ]   the Division of Child Support provides support enforcement services for this case [see 3.11] and there is good cause [as stated below under "Good Cause"] not to require immediate income withholding which is in the best interests of the child and, in modification cases, previously ordered child support has been timely paid:

[ ] the Division of Child Support does not provide support enforcement services for this case [see 3.11] and there is good cause [as stated below under "Good Cause"] not to require immediate income withholding:

Good Cause:

3.13   TERMINATION OF SUPPORT.

Support shall be paid:

[ ]   provided that this is a temporary order, until a subsequent child support order is entered by this court.

[ ]   until the child(ren) reach(es) the age of 18, except as otherwise provided below in Paragraph 3.14.

[X]   until the child(ren) reach(es) the age of 18 or as long as the child(ren) remain(s) enrolled in high school, whichever occurs last, except as otherwise provided below in Paragraph 3.14.

[ ]   after the age of 18 for _____ [Name] who is a dependent adult child, until the child is capable of self-support and the necessity for support ceases.

[ ]   until the obligation for post secondary support set forth in Paragraph 3.14 begins for the child(ren).

[ ]   Other:

3.14   POST SECONDARY EDUCATIONAL SUPPORT.

[ ]   No post secondary educational support shall be required.

[X]   The right to petition for post secondary support is reserved, provided that the right is exercised before support terminates as set forth in paragraph 3.13.

[ ]   The parents shall pay for the post secondary educational support of the child(ren). Post secondary support provisions will be decided by agreement or by the court.

[ ]   Other:

3.15   PAYMENT FOR EXPENSES NOT INCLUDED IN THE TRANSFER PAYMENT.

[ ]   Does not apply because all payments, except medical, are included in the transfer payment.

[ ]   The mother shall pay _____% and the father _____% (each parent's proportional share of income from the Child Support Schedule Worksheet, line 6) of the following expenses incurred on behalf of the children listed in Paragraph 3.1:

    [ ]   day care.

    [ ]   educational expenses.

    [ ]   long distance transportation expenses.

    [ ]   other:

Payments shall be made to [ ] the provider of the service [ ] the parent receiving the transfer payment.

[ ] The obligor shall pay the following amounts each month the expense is incurred on behalf of the children listed in Paragraph 3.1:

    [ ] day care: $ _____ payable to the [ ] day care provider [ ] other parent;

    [ ] educational expenses: $ _____ payable to the [ ] educational provider [ ] other parent;

    [ ] long distance transportation: $ _____ payable to the [ ] transportation provider [ ] other parent.

    [ ] other:

3.16 PERIODIC ADJUSTMENT.

    [ ] Does not apply.

    [X] Child support shall be adjusted periodically as follows:

    Both parties are required to provide the other with income tax returns for the preceeding two years on the first day of May of every even numbered year for the purpose of recalculating support for the two years to follow.

    [ ] Other:

3.17 INCOME TAX EXEMPTIONS.

    [ ] Does not apply.

    [X] Tax exemptions for the children shall be allocated as follows:

    To the Petitioner.

    [ ] The parents shall sign the federal income tax dependency exemption waiver.

    [ ] Other:

3.18 MEDICAL INSURANCE FOR THE CHILDREN LISTED IN PARAGRAPH 3.1.

Unless one or more of the boxes below are checked, each parent shall maintain or provide health insurance coverage if:

(a) Coverage that can be extended to cover the child(ren) is or becomes available to each parent through employment or is union-related; and

(b) The cost of such coverage for the mother does not exceed $_____ (25 percent of mother's basic child support obligation on Worksheet Line 7), and the cost of such coverage for the father does not exceed $_____ (25 percent of father's basic child support obligation on Worksheet Line 7).

SAMPLE 25—Continued

[ ] The parent below shall maintain or provide health insurance coverage if coverage that can be extended to cover the child(ren) is or becomes available to that parent through employment or is union-related and the cost of such coverage does not exceed $_____ (25 percent of that parent's basic child support obligation on Worksheet Line 7).

    [ ] Mother
    [ ] Father

[ ] The parent below shall maintain or provide health insurance coverage if coverage that can be extended to cover the child(ren) is or becomes available to that parent through employment or is union-related even if such coverage exceeds $_____ (25 percent of that parent's basic child support obligation on Worksheet Line 7).

    [ ] Mother
    [ ] Father

[ ] The parent below is not obligated to provide health insurance coverage:

    [ ] Mother
    [ ] Father

This parent is not obligated to provide health insurance coverage because:

    [ ] The other parent provides insurance coverage
    [ ] Other:

The parent(s) shall maintain health insurance coverage, if available for the children listed in paragraph 3.1, until further order of the court or until health insurance is no longer available through the parents' employer or union and no conversion privileges exist to continue coverage following termination of employment.

A parent who is required under this order to provide health insurance coverage is liable for any covered health care costs for which that parent receives direct payment from an insurer.

A parent who is required under this order to provide health insurance coverage shall provide proof that such coverage is available or not available within 20 days of the entry of this order to the physical custodian or the Washington State Support Registry if the parent has been notified or ordered to make payments to the Washington State Support Registry.

If proof that health insurance coverage is available or not available is not provided within 20 days, the obligee or the Department of Social and Health Services may seek direct enforcement of the coverage through the obligor's employer or union without further notice to the obligor as provided under Chapter 26.18 RCW.

3.19   EXTRAORDINARY HEALTH CARE EXPENSES.

The OBLIGOR shall pay ___50___ % of extraordinary health care expenses (the obligor's proportional share of income from the Child Support Schedule Worksheet, line 6), if monthly medical expenses exceed $ _____ (5% of the basic support obligation from Worksheet line 5).

3.20   BACK CHILD SUPPORT.

    ☒   No back child support is owed at this time.

[ ]   Back child support that may be owed is not affected by this order.

[ ]   The obligee parent is awarded a judgment against the obligor parent in the amount of $ _____ for back child support for the period from _____ [Date] to _____ [Date].

[ ]   Other:

3.21   BACK INTEREST.

[X]   No back interest is owed at this time.

[ ]   Back interest that may be owed is not affected by this order.

[ ]   The obligee parent is awarded a judgment against the obligor parent in the amount of $ _____ for back interest for the period from _____ [Date] to _____ [Date].

[ ]   Other:

3.22   OTHER:

Dated: _4/12/200-_____   *J.M. Judge*_____
                                                    Judge/Commissioner

Presented by: Approved for entry:
                                           Notice of presentation waived:

*Sue Snoopie*_____   _____
Signature   Signature

SUE SNOOPIE_____   _____
Print or Type Name   Print or Type Name

[X]   I apply for full support enforcement services from the DSHS Division of Child Support.

       *Sue Snoopie*_____
       Signature of Party

[ ]   Approved for entry in Public Assistance cases, notice of presentation waived.

       _____
       Deputy Prosecuting Attorney

ORDER OF CHILD SUPPORT (ORS) - Page 10 of 10
WPF DR 01.0500 (9/2001) - RCW 26.09.175; 26.26.132(5)   SELF-COUNSEL PRESS – DIV WA (22-10) 01

112

SAMPLE 26
NOTE FOR DISSOLUTION CALENDAR

SUPERIOR COURT OF WASHINGTON
COUNTY OF SPOKANE

In re the Marriage of:

SUE SNOOPIE

Petitioner,

and

SAM SNOOPIE

Respondent.

NO. XX-X-XXXXX-X

NOTE FOR DISSOLUTION CALENDAR
(NON-CONTESTED CASE - OPTION
USE)
(NTC)
Clerk's Action Required

TO THE CLERK OF COURT AND TO:

1.   Please note that this case will be placed on the non-contested dissolution calendar for hearing on the date set out below.

2.   A hearing has been set for the following date, time and place.

Date: APRIL 12, 200-   Time: 9:30   a.m./~~p.m.~~
Place: SPOKANE COUNTY COURTHOUSE   Room/Department: ROOM 300

Dated: MARCH 20, 200-   *Sue Snoopie*
                                 Signature of Lawyer or Party

                                 SUE SNOOPIE
                                 Print or Type Name
                                 Notice to party: you may list an address that is not your
                                 residential address where you agree to accept legal documents.

                                 _____
                                 Address
                                 _____

SUPERIOR COURT OF WASHINGTON
COUNTY OF SPOKANE

In re the Marriage of:
 	
SUE SNOOPIE
 	
                                       Petitioner,
and
 	
SAM SNOOPIE
 	
                                    Respondent.
	NO. XX-X-XXXXX-X
	
	FINDINGS OF FACT AND
	CONCLUSIONS OF LAW
	(FNFCL)

I. BASIS FOR FINDINGS

The findings are based on:

[ ]   agreement.
[X]   an order of default entered on   12/24/200-   [Date].
[ ]   trial. The following people attended:

        [X]   Petitioner.
        [ ]   Petitioner's Lawyer.
        [ ]   Respondent.
        [ ]   Respondent's Lawyer.
        [ ]   Other:

II. FINDINGS OF FACT

Upon the basis of the court record, the court FINDS:

2.1   RESIDENCY OF PETITIONER.

    The petitioner

        [X]   is a resident of the state of Washington.
        [ ]   is not a resident of the state of Washington.
        [ ]   is a member of the armed forces and has been stationed in this state for at least 90 days.

2.2   NOTICE TO THE RESPONDENT.

    The respondent

        [ ]   appeared, responded or joined in the petition.

    ☒   was served in the following manner:
               Personally served on 01/11/200- at 2:30 p.m. at 111 2nd St. Yakima, WA
               99201

2.3   BASIS OF PERSONAL JURISDICTION OVER THE RESPONDENT.

    [ ]   There are no facts to establish personal jurisdiction over the respondent.

    ☒   The facts below establish personal jurisdiction over the respondent.

        ☒   The respondent is presently residing in Washington.
        [ ]   The parties lived in Washington during their marriage and the petitioner continues to reside, or be a member of the armed forces stationed, in this state.
        [ ]   The parties may have conceived a child while within Washington.
        [ ]   Other:

2.4   DATE AND PLACE OF MARRIAGE.

    The parties were married on 7/2/89   [Date] at   SEATTLE, WA   [Place].

2.5   STATUS OF THE PARTIES.

    ☒   Husband and wife separated on   03/01/200-   [Date].

    [ ]   Husband and wife are not separated.

2.6   STATUS OF THE MARRIAGE.

    ☒   The marriage is irretrievably broken and at least 90 days have elapsed since the date the petition was filed and since the date the summons was served or the respondent joined.

    [ ]   The petitioner wishes to be legally separated.

    [ ]   The petitioner is petitioning for a declaration concerning the invalidity of the marriage. The court FINDS the following facts concerning the validity of the marriage:

2.7   SEPARATION CONTRACT OR PRENUPTIAL AGREEMENT.

    ☒   There is no written separation contract or prenuptial agreement.

[ ]   A written separation contract or prenuptial agreement was executed on
_____ [Date] and is filed herein.

    [ ]   The separation contract should be approved.

    [ ]   The separation contract should not be approved because:

[ ]   Other:

2.8   COMMUNITY PROPERTY.

[ ]   The parties do not have real or personal community property.
[ ]   The parties have real or personal community property as set forth in Exhibit _____. This exhibit is attached or filed and incorporated by reference as part of these findings.
[X]   The parties have the following real or personal community property:

House at 123 Beagle St., Spokane, Washington
1998 Taurus car
1995 Buick car
Bank account at Washington Mutual (Wife's)
Wife's pension at Acme Widget Co.
Husband's pension at XYZ Corp.
Bank account at Seattle First (Husband's)

[ ]   Other:

2.9   SEPARATE PROPERTY.

[X]   The husband has no real or personal separate property.

[X]   The wife has no real or personal separate property.

[ ]   The husband has real or personal separate property as set forth in Exhibit _____. This exhibit is attached or filed and incorporated by reference as part of these findings.

[ ]   The wife has real or personal separate property as set forth in Exhibit _____. This exhibit is attached or filed and incorporated by reference as part of these findings.

[ ]   The husband has the following real or personal separate property:

[ ] The wife has the following real or personal separate property:

[ ] Other:

2.10 COMMUNITY LIABILITIES.

[ ] There are no known community liabilities.

[ ] The parties have incurred community liabilities as set forth in Exhibit _____. This exhibit is attached or filed and incorporated by reference as part of these findings.

[X] The parties have incurred the following community liabilities:

Creditor	Amount
Nordstrom	$ 500
Seafirst Mastercard	$ 200
Visa	$2,000
Credit Union Loan	$1,000

[ ] Other:

2.11 SEPARATE LIABILITIES.

[X] The husband has no known separate liabilities.

[X] The wife has no known separate liabilities.

[ ] The husband has incurred separate liabilities as set forth in Exhibit _____. This exhibit is attached or filed and incorporated by reference as part of these findings.

[ ] The wife has incurred separate liabilities as set forth in Exhibit _____. This exhibit is attached or filed and incorporated by reference as part of these findings.

SAMPLE 27—Continued

[ ]   The husband has incurred the following separate liabilities:

        <u>Creditor</u>   <u>Amount</u>

[ ]   The wife has incurred the following separate liabilities:

        <u>Creditor</u>   <u>Amount</u>

[ ]   Other:

2.12   MAINTENANCE.

    ☒   Maintenance was not requested.

    [ ]   Maintenance should not be ordered because:

    [ ]   Maintenance should be ordered because:

    [ ]   Other:

2.13   CONTINUING RESTRAINING ORDER.

    ☒   Does not apply.

[ ]   A continuing restraining order against the [ ] husband [ ] wife [ ] both parties is necessary because:

[ ]   Other:

2.14   FEES AND COSTS.

       ☒   There is no award of fees or costs because:

       [ ]   The [ ] husband [ ] wife has the need for the payment of fees and costs and the other spouse has the ability to pay these fees and costs. The [ ] husband [ ] wife has incurred reasonable attorney fees and costs in the amount of $_____.

       [ ]   Other:

2.15   PREGNANCY.

       ☒   The wife is not pregnant.

       [ ]   The wife is pregnant. The father of the unborn child is [ ] the husband [ ] not the husband [ ] undetermined.

       [ ]   Other:

2.16   DEPENDENT CHILDREN.

       [ ]   The parties have no dependent children of this marriage.

       ☒   The children listed below are dependent upon either or both spouses.

Name of Child	Age	Mother's Name	Father's Name
SUSIE SNOOPIE	10	SUE SNOOPIE	SAM SNOOPIE

       [ ]   Other:

2.17   JURISDICTION OVER THE CHILDREN.

    [ ]   Does not apply because there are no dependent children.

    [ ]   This court does not have jurisdiction over the children.

    [X]   This court has jurisdiction over the children for the reasons set forth below.

        [ ]   This court has exclusive continuing jurisdiction. The court has previously made a child custody, parenting plan, residential schedule or visitation determination in this matter and retains jurisdiction under RCW 26.27.211.

        [X]   This state is the home state of the children because:

            [X]   the children lived in Washington with a parent or a person acting as a parent for at least six consecutive months immediately preceding the commencement of this proceeding.

            [ ]   the children are less than six months old and have lived in Washington with a parent or a person acting as parent since birth.

            [ ]   any absences from Washington have been only temporary.

            [ ]   Washington was the home state of the children within six months before the commencement of this proceeding and the children are absent from the state but a parent or person acting as a parent continued to live in this state.

        [ ]   The children and the parents or the children and at least one parent or person acting as a parent, have significant connection with the state other than mere physical presence; and substantial evidence is available in this state concerning the children's care, protection, training and personal relationships; and

            [ ]   the children have no home state elsewhere.

            [ ]   the children's home state has declined to exercise jurisdiction on the ground that this state is the more appropriate forum under RCW 26.27.261 or .271.

        [ ]   All courts in the children's home state have declined to exercise jurisdiction on the ground that a court of this state is the more appropriate forum to determine the custody of the children under RCW 26.27.261 or .271.

        [ ]   No other state has jurisdiction.

        [ ]   This court has temporary emergency jurisdiction over this proceeding because the children are present in this state and the children have been abandoned or it is necessary in an emergency to protect the children because the children, or a sibling or parent of the children is subjected to or threatened with abuse. RCW 26.27.231.

    [ ]   Other:

2.18   PARENTING PLAN.

    [ ]   Does not apply.

    [X]   The parenting plan signed by the court on ____(date of hearing)____ [Date] is approved and incorporated as part of these findings.

        [ ]   This parenting plan is the result of an agreement of the parties.

[ ]   Other:

2.19   CHILD SUPPORT.

[ ]   Does not apply.

[X]   There are children in need of support and child support should be set pursuant to the Washington
        State Child Support Schedule. The Order of Child Support signed by the court on
        _____(date of hearing)_____[Date] and the child support worksheet, which has been
        approved by the court, are incorporated by reference in these findings.

[ ]   Other:

2.20   OTHER.

III. CONCLUSIONS OF LAW

The court makes the following conclusions of law from the foregoing findings of fact:

3.1   JURISDICTION.

[X]   The court has jurisdiction to enter a decree in this matter.

[ ]   Other:

3.2   GRANTING OF A DECREE.

[X]   The parties should be granted a decree.

[ ]   Other:

3.3   DISPOSITION.

The court should determine the marital status of the parties, make provision for a parenting plan for any
minor children of the marriage, make provision for the support of any minor child of the marriage entitled
to support, consider or approve provision for the maintenance of either spouse, make provision for the
disposition of property and liabilities of the parties, make provision for the allocation of the children as
federal tax exemptions, make provision for any necessary continuing restraining orders, and make
provision for the change of name of any party. The distribution of property and liabilities as set forth in
the decree is fair and equitable.

FNDNGS OF FACT AND CONCL OF LAW (FNFCL) – Page 8 of 9
WPF DR 04.0300 (9/2001) - CR 52; RCW 26.09.030; .070 (3)   SELF-COUNSEL PRESS – DIV WA (11-8) 01

3.4   CONTINUING RESTRAINING ORDER.

      [X]   Does not apply.
      [ ]   A continuing restraining order should be entered.

3.5   ATTORNEY'S FEES AND COSTS.

      [X]   Does not apply.
      [ ]   Attorney's fees, other professional fees and costs should be paid.

3.6   OTHER.

Dated: _____04/12/200-_____   _____*J.M. Judge*_____
                                      Judge/Commissioner

Presented by: Approved for entry:
                                      Notice of presentation waived:

_____*Sue Snoopie*_____   _____
Signature   Signature

_____SUE SNOOPIE_____   _____
Print or Type Name   Print or Type Name

FNDNGS OF FACT AND CONCL OF LAW (FNFCL) - Page 9 of 9
WPF DR 04.0300 (9/2001) - CR 52; RCW 26.09.030; .070 (3)

SELF-COUNSEL PRESS – DIV WA (11-9) 01

SAMPLE 28
DECREE OF DISSOLUTION

SUPERIOR COURT OF WASHINGTON
COUNTY OF SPOKANE

In re the Marriage of:

SUE SNOOPIE

                            Petitioner,

and

SAM SNOOPIE

                            Respondent.

NO.   XX-X-XXXXX-X

[X]   DECREE OF DISSOLUTION (DCD)
[ ]   DECREE OF LEGAL SEPARATION
      (DCLGSP)
[ ]   DECLARATION CONCERNING
      VALIDITY (DCINMG)

[ ] Clerk's action required

I. JUDGMENT/ORDER SUMMARIES

1.1 RESTRAINING ORDER SUMMARY:

    [X] Does not apply.   [ ] Restraining Order Summary is set forth below:

Name of person(s) restrained: _____. Name of person(s) protected:_____. **See paragraph 3.8.**

VIOLATION OF A RESTRAINING ORDER IN PARAGRAPH 3.8 BELOW WITH ACTUAL KNOWLEDGE OF ITS TERMS IS A CRIMINAL OFFENSE UNDER CHAPTER 26.50 RCW AND WILL SUBJECT THE VIOLATOR TO ARREST. RCW 26.09.050.

1.2 REAL PROPERTY JUDGMENT SUMMARY:

    [X] Does not apply.   [ ] Real Property Judgment Summary is set forth below:

Assessor's property tax parcel or account number:		
Or		
Legal description of the property awarded (including lot, block, plat, or section, township, range, county and state):		
	See Page	for full legal description

1.3 MONEY JUDGMENT SUMMARY:

    ☒ Does not apply. [ ] Judgment Summary is set forth below.

A. Judgment creditor   _____
B. Judgment debtor   _____
C. Principal judgment amount $ _____
D. Interest to date of judgment $ _____
E. Attorney's fees $ _____
F. Costs $ _____
G. Other recovery amount $ _____
H. Principal judgment shall bear interest at _____ % per annum
I. Attorney's fees, costs and other recovery amounts shall bear interest at _____ % per annum
J. Attorney for judgment creditor   _____
K. Attorney for judgment debtor   _____
L. Other:

END OF SUMMARIES

II. BASIS

Findings of Fact and Conclusions of Law have been entered in this case.

III. DECREE

IT IS DECREED that:

3.1 STATUS OF THE MARRIAGE.

    ☒   The marriage of the parties is dissolved.
    [ ]   The husband and wife are legally separated.
    [ ]   The marriage of the parties is invalid.
    [ ]   The marriage of the parties is valid.

3.2 PROPERTY TO BE AWARDED THE HUSBAND.

    [ ]   Does not apply.
    [ ]   The husband is awarded as his separate property the property set forth in Exhibit _____. This exhibit is attached or filed and incorporated by reference as part of this decree.
    ☒   The husband is awarded as his separate property the following property (list real estate, furniture, vehicles, pensions, insurance, bank accounts, etc.):

         His pension at XYZ Corp.
         1995 Buick
         His bank account

SAMPLE 28—Continued

[ ]   Other:

3.3   PROPERTY TO BE AWARDED TO THE WIFE.

[ ]   Does not apply.
[ ]   The wife is awarded as her separate property the property set forth in Exhibit _____. This
       exhibit is attached or filed and incorporated by reference as part of this decree.
[X]   The wife is awarded as her separate property the following property (list real estate, furniture,
       vehicles, pensions, insurance, bank accounts, etc.):

       A house at North 123 Beagle Street, Spokane, WA
       1998 Taurus car
       Her bank accounts
       The furniture in the family home
       Her pension at Acme Widget Co.

[ ]   Other:

3.4   LIABILITIES TO BE PAID BY THE HUSBAND.

[ ]   Does not apply.
[ ]   The husband shall pay the community or separate liabilities set forth in Exhibit _____. This
       exhibit is attached or filed and incorporated by reference as part of this decree.
[X]   The husband shall pay the following community or separate liabilities:

Creditor	Amount
Visa	$2,000
Credit Union Loan	$1,000

[ ]   Other:

DECREE (DCD) (DCLSP) (DCINMG) - Page 3 of 6
WPF DR 04.0400 (9/2001) - RCW 26.09.030; .040; .070 (3)   SELF-COUNSEL PRESS – DIV WA (12-3) 01

125

Unless otherwise provided herein, the husband shall pay all liabilities incurred by him since the date of separation.

3.5   LIABILITIES TO BE PAID BY THE WIFE.

[ ]   Does not apply.
[ ]   The wife shall pay the community or separate liabilities set forth in Exhibit _____ . This exhibit is attached or filed and incorporated by reference as part of this decree.
[X]   The wife shall pay the following community or separate liabilities:

Creditor	Amount
Nordstrom	$500
Seafirst Mastercard	$200

[ ]   Other:

Unless otherwise provided herein, the wife shall pay all liabilities incurred by her since the date of separation.

3.6   HOLD HARMLESS PROVISION.

[ ]   Does not apply.
[X]   Each party shall hold the other party harmless from any collection action relating to separate or community liabilities set forth above, including reasonable attorney's fees and costs incurred in defending against any attempts to collect an obligation of the other party.
[ ]   Other:

3.7   SPOUSAL MAINTENANCE.

[X]   Does not apply.
[ ]   The [ ] husband [ ] wife shall pay maintenance as set forth in Exhibit _____ . This exhibit is attached or filed and incorporated by reference as part of this decree.
[ ]   The [ ] husband [ ] wife shall pay $ _____ maintenance. Maintenance shall be paid [ ] weekly [ ] semi-monthly [ ] monthly.
        The first maintenance payment shall be due on _____ [Date].

The obligation to pay future maintenance is terminated upon the death of either party or the remarriage of the party receiving maintenance unless otherwise specified below:

Payments shall be made:

    [ ]   directly to the other spouse.

    [ ]   to the Washington State Child Support Registry (only available if child support is ordered).

    [ ]   to the clerk of this court as trustee for remittance to the other spouse (only available if there are no dependent children).

[ ]   If a spousal maintenance payment is more than 15 days past due and the total of such past due payments is equal to or greater than $100, or if the obligor requests a withdrawal of accumulated contributions from the Department of Retirement Systems, the obligee may seek a mandatory benefits assignment order under Chapter 41.50 RCW without prior notice to the obligor.

[ ]   The Department of Retirement Systems may make a direct payment of all or part of a withdrawal of accumulated contributions pursuant to RCW 41.50.550(3).

[ ]   Other:

3.8   CONTINUING RESTRAINING ORDER.

    ☒   Does not apply.

    [ ]   A continuing restraining order is entered as follows:

        [ ]   The [ ] husband [ ] wife is restrained and enjoined from assaulting, harassing, molesting or disturbing the peace of the other party.

        [ ]   The [ ] husband [ ] wife is restrained and enjoined from going onto the grounds of or entering the home, work place or school of the other party, or the day care or school of the following named children: _____

                _____

        [ ]   The [ ] husband [ ] wife is restrained and enjoined from knowingly coming within or knowingly remaining within _____(distance) of the home, work place or school of the other party, or the day care or school of these children:

                _____ .

                other:_____ .

        [ ]   Other:

VIOLATION OF A RESTRAINING ORDER IN PARAGRAPH 3.8 WITH ACTUAL KNOWLEDGE OF ITS TERMS IS A CRIMINAL OFFENSE UNDER CHAPTER 26.50 RCW AND WILL SUBJECT THE VIOLATOR TO ARREST. RCW 26.09.060.

    [ ]   CLERK'S ACTION. The clerk of the court shall forward a copy of this order, on or before the next judicial day, to: _____ law enforcement agency which shall enter this order into any computer-based criminal intelligence system available in this state used by law enforcement agencies to list outstanding warrants. (**A law enforcement information sheet must be completed by the party or the party's attorney and provided with this order before this order will be entered into the law enforcement computer system.**)

EXPIRATION.

This restraining order expires on: _____ (month/day/year).

This restraining order supersedes all previous temporary restraining orders in this cause number.

3.9   JURISDICTION OVER THE CHILDREN.

    [ ]   Does not apply because there are no dependent children.

DECREE (DCD) (DCLSP) (DCINMG) - Page 5 of 6
WPF DR 04.0400 (9/2001) - RCW 26.09.030; .040; .070 (3)   SELF-COUNSEL PRESS – DIV WA (12-5) 01

127

[X]   The court has jurisdiction over the children as set forth in the Findings of Fact and Conclusions of Law.

3.10   PARENTING PLAN.

[ ]   Does not apply.
[X]   The parties shall comply with the Parenting Plan signed by the court on ___(date of hearing)___ [Date]. The Parenting Plan signed by the court is approved and incorporated as part of this decree.

3.11   CHILD SUPPORT.

[ ]   Does not apply.
[X]   Child support shall be paid in accordance with the order of child support signed by the court on ___(date of hearing)___ [Date]. This order is incorporated as part of this decree.

3.12   ATTORNEY'S FEES, OTHER PROFESSIONAL FEES AND COSTS.

[X]   Does not apply.
[ ]   Attorney's fees, other professional fees and costs shall be paid as follows:

3.13   NAME CHANGES.

[ ]   Does not apply.
[X]   The wife's name shall be changed to ___SUE SMITH___ [Name].
[ ]   The husband's name shall be changed to _____ [Name].

3.14   OTHER.

Dated: ___04/12/200-___   *J.M. Judge*
                                     JUDGE/COMMISSIONER

Presented by: Approved for entry:
                                                  Notice for presentation waived:

Sue Snoopie
Signature   Signature

SUE SNOOPIE
Print or Type Name   Print or Type Name

DECREE (DCD) (DCLSP) (DCINMG) - Page 6 of 6
WPF DR 04.0400 (9/2001) - RCW 26.09.030; .040; .070 (3)   SELF-COUNSEL PRESS – DIV WA (12-6) 01

128

WAIVER OF RIGHTS UNDER SOLDIERS AND SAILORS' CIVIL RELIEF ACT AND ADMISSION OF SERVICE

SUPERIOR COURT OF WASHINGTON
COUNTY OF SPOKANE

In re the Marriage of:

SUE SNOOPIE

Petitioner,

and

SAM SNOOPIE

Respondent.

NO. XX-X-XXXXX-X

WAIVER OF RIGHTS UNDER SOLDIERS
AND SAILORS' CIVIL RELIEF ACT AND
ADMISSION OF SERVICE

My name is SAM SNOOPIE and I am the above-named Respondent.
My spouse has petitioned the above-entitled court to terminate our marriage under the laws of the state of
Washington. I am a member of the United States military service and I am informed of my rights under the Soldiers
and Sailors' Civil Relief Act of March 4, 1918, as amended. I do hereby waive my rights under the Soldiers and
Sailors' Civil Relief Act and I request the court to terminate our marriage as requested by the Petitioner.

I received a copy of the Summons and Petition in this matter as issued by the court under the above case number on
the 3rd day of March , 200- .

I admit and acknowledge service of process upon me in this matter.

Sam Snoopie
(Signature)

Name: SAM SNOOPIE

Rank: CORPORAL

Serial Number: 98765-432

Unit: 007

Subscribed and sworn to before me this 10th day of March , 20 0- .

J.G. Advocate
Judge Advocate

SELF-COUNSEL PRESS – DIV WA (19-1) 01

5
MISCELLANEOUS MATTERS

a. IF YOUR SPOUSE IS MISSING, OR YOU CANNOT AFFORD A PROCESS SERVER, OR YOUR SPOUSE IS OUT OF STATE

1. Service by publication

If you do not know where your spouse is, you may be able to serve him or her by publication. In order to do that you have to get a judge's signature on an order. The forms for publishing are:

(a) Form DR 01.0260, Declaration for Service of Summons by Publication, (see Sample 30),

(b) Form DR 01.0265, Order for Service of Summons by Publication, (see Sample 31), and

(c) Form DR 01.0270, Summons by Publication, (see Sample 32.) (This form must be published in a newspaper).

Be warned: you will not be able to get what is called "personal relief" by this process. That is, you will not be awarded any property, child support, or maintenance; only the dissolution of your marriage and custody of the children are settled by this process.

2. Service by mail

Service by mail is an alternative in the following circumstances:

(a) Your spouse lives out of state,

(b) Your spouse has consistently avoided personal service,

(c) You have no friend or relative who could serve your spouse, or

(d) You don't have the money for an out-of-state server.

Samples 33, 34, and 35 show how you would prepare the forms in this case.

b. IF YOU HAVE WAITED MORE THAN A YEAR BETWEEN DATE OF PETITION AND PROCEEDING WITH YOUR DIVORCE

If more than a year has elapsed between your filing of the Petition and the continuation of your divorce, you will have to show the court that you have given your spouse notice of your intention to proceed.

If you served your spouse the Petition with a Summons, and he or she did not respond, you must send a copy of the Notice of Taking Default and Entry of Decree of Dissolution After One Year (see Sample 36).

The original Notice of Taking Default and Entry of Decree of Dissolution After One Year should be given to the county clerk, who will place it in your file. When you receive the return receipt with your spouse's signature from the post office, attach it to the Declaration of Mailing (Notice of Taking Default) (see Sample 37).

You must take the Declaration of Mailing with you when you go to court for your Decree of Dissolution as proof of notice to your spouse of the re-commencement of the divorce proceedings.

c. HOW TO DISCONTINUE YOUR DIVORCE

If you have reconciled with your spouse or if you decide for any reason that you cannot go through with the divorce, there are two ways to stop the court proceedings:

(a) If you do nothing more, the county clerk will dismiss the action after a year.

(b) You may fill out a Motion for Non-Suit and Order of Dismissal (see Sample 38) and take it to the courthouse. Ask the county clerk for your file and take your file to the presiding judge or commissioner. Present the judge or commissioner with the Motion for Non-Suit and Order for Dismissal and explain that you want to discontinue your divorce. The judge will sign the form and your case will be dismissed. Return the divorce file to the county clerk.

Once your case has been dismissed, if you should ever wish to begin divorce proceedings again, you will have to begin from the beginning by filing a new Petition and paying the filing fee. The county clerk will open a new court file and give you a new number.

d. HOW TO APPLY FOR FINANCIAL AID

As stated earlier in this book, when you begin your divorce proceedings by filing your Petition for Dissolution of the Marriage and your Summons (required if you and your spouse are not filing jointly), you must pay a filing fee to the county clerk.

If paying this fee would be a financial hardship to you, you may apply to the court to have this fee waived. If your spouse lives outside Washington, the court may also allow you to serve your spouse by certified mail rather than having the expense of service by sheriff.

The procedure by which you ask for this financial consideration is called In Forma Pauperis. First you fill out your Petition and Summons as outlined previously in this book. Then you fill out a Motion and Declaration for Order to Commence and Prosecute Proceeding In Forma Pauperis (see Sample 39). You also fill out an Order Authorizing Proceeding In Forma Pauperis (see Sample 40).

Next, take these forms to the courthouse and ask the county clerk which judge or court commissioner is authorized to sign your Order and Motion for Proceeding In Forma Pauperis. Then go to that judge or court commissioner's courtroom and ask for the bailiff. Show the bailiff your papers: the Order Authorizing Proceedings In Forma Pauperis should be on top, the Motion and Declaration for Order to Commence and Prosecute Proceeding In Forma Pauperis should be next, and the Summons and Petition should be third and fourth.

The bailiff will take you before the judge or court commissioner and will hand your forms to him or her. You should then give the court commissioner the following information:

(a) Your name and address, as well as your spouse's

(b) The fact that you intend to terminate the marriage because it is irretrievably broken

(c) The fact that you do not have the funds to pay the filing fees or the notary fees for your Petition

(d) Ask the court to sign your motion to proceed In Forma Pauperis

You may wish to write this information out in a politely worded paragraph and read it to the judge or court commissioner. He or she will then ask you some questions about your financial situation. If your funds are limited and barely meet your living costs, the court may decide that you cannot afford the court costs.

After the judge signs your Motion and Order In Forma Pauperis, take all your papers to the county clerk. He or she will stamp them "filed," and give you your case number.

If your spouse lives outside Washington, and you know the address, ask the court for permission to serve the Summons and Petition by certified mail rather than through a sheriff or process server in another state. This will save you cost of service.

When you receive the return receipt with your spouse's signature from the post office, fill out the Declaration of Mailing (see Sample 41) and attach the return receipt to it. Sign the Declaration of Mailing and take it to the county clerk for filing.

SUPERIOR COURT OF WASHINGTON
COUNTY OF SPOKANE

In re the Marriage of:

SUE SNOOPIE

                         Petitioner,

and

SAM SNOOPIE

                         Respondent.

NO. XX-X-XXXXX-X

MOTION AND DECLARATION FOR
SERVICE OF SUMMONS BY
PUBLICATION
(DCLR)

I. MOTION

The petitioner moves the court, pursuant to RCW 4.28.100, for an order allowing service of the summons and petition by publication.

Dated: 03/30/200-   *Sue Snoopie*
                                          Signature of Lawyer or Petitioner

                                          SUE SNOOPIE
                                          Print or Type Name

II. DECLARATION

2.1.   Service of summons by publication is justified because:

    [X]   the respondent is not a resident of this state.
    [ ]   the respondent cannot be found in this state because:

        [ ]   the respondent has departed from Washington to avoid service of summons.
        [ ]   the respondent has concealed himself/herself to avoid service of summons.
        [X]   other:
            He is originally from the midwest but none of his friends know
            where he is.

2.2   The facts supporting the above allegations are:

2.3.   The following efforts were made to locate the respondent for personal service or service by mail:

         I have made careful inquiry of relations friends, and business associates of the Respondent and I cannot learn of his present whereabouts. I know of no address to which I could mail the Summons to the Respondent. The following are the names of the persons whom I have contacted: Emily Snoopie, John Jackson, Bob Sneaky.

2.4.   [ ]   A copy of the summons (substantially in the form prescribed in RCW 4.28.110) and the petition have been deposited in the post office, directed to the respondent at the respondent's place of residence.

         [X]   I do not know the respondent's address.

I declare under penalty of perjury under the laws of the state of Washington that the foregoing is true and correct.

Signed at <u>SPOKANE, WASHINGTON</u> , on <u>03/30/200-</u>   .
                [Place]   [Date]

                                   Sue Snoopie
                                   Signature

                                   SUE SNOOPIE
                                   Print or Type Name

MOT AND DECL FOR SERV BY PUBLICATION (DCLR) - Page 2 of 2
WPF DR 01.0260 (9/2000) - RCW 4.28.100, CR 4   SELF-COUNSEL PRESS – DIV WA (13-2) 01

135

SUPERIOR COURT OF WASHINGTON
COUNTY OF SPOKANE

In re the Marriage of:

SUE SNOOPIE

Petitioner,

and

SAM SNOOPIE

Respondent.

NO. XX-X-XXXXX-X

ORDER FOR SERVICE OF SUMMONS
BY PUBLICATION
(If Required by Local Practice)
(ORPUB)

I. BASIS

The court has considered a motion and declaration requesting that the summons in this matter be served on the respondent by publication.

II. FINDINGS

Based on the representations made in the declaration, the court FINDS that the summons in this matter may be served on the respondent by publication in accordance with RCW 4.28.100.

III. ORDER

IT IS ORDERED that the summons in this matter may be served on the respondent by publication in conformity with RCW 4.28.100.

Dated: March 30, 200-

J.M. Judge
Judge/Commissioner

Presented by:

Sue Snoopie
Signature

SUE SNOOPIE
Print or Type Name

SUPERIOR COURT OF WASHINGTON
COUNTY OF SPOKANE

In re the Marriage of:

SUE SNOOPIE

                                         Petitioner,

and

SAM SNOOPIE

                                      Respondent.

NO. X-XX-XXXXX-X

SUMMONS BY
PUBLICATION
(SMPB)

TO THE RESPONDENT:

[NOTE TO PUBLISHER: Publish only those boxes which are checked.]

1.   The petitioner has started an action in the above court requesting:

        [X]   that your marriage be dissolved.
        [ ]   a legal separation.
        [ ]   that the validity of your marriage be determined.

2.   The petition also requests that the court grant the following relief:

        [ ]   Provide reasonable maintenance for the [ ] husband [ ] wife.
        [X]   Approve a parenting plan for the dependent children.
        [X]   Determine support for the dependent children pursuant to the Washington State Support Schedule.
        [ ]   Approve a separation agreement.
        [X]   Dispose of property and liabilities.
        [X]   Change name of wife to: SUE SMITH   .
        [ ]   Change name of husband to: .
        [ ]   Order payment of court costs and reasonable fees.
        [ ]   Enter a continuing restraining order.
        [ ]   Order payment of day care expenses for the children.
        [X]   Award the tax exemptions for the dependent children as follows:

                TO THE PETITIONER

        [ ]   Order payment of attorney's fees, other professional fees and costs.
        [ ]   Other:

3. You must respond to this summons by serving a copy of your written response on the person signing this summons and by filing the original with the clerk of the court. If you do not serve your written response within 60 days after the date of the first publication of this summons (60 days after the 30th day of March , 200-), the court may enter an order of default against you, and the court may, without further notice to you, enter a decree and approve or provide for other relief requested in this summons. In the case of a dissolution of marriage, the court will not enter the final decree until at least 90 days after service and filing. If you serve a notice of appearance on the undersigned person, you are entitled to notice before an order of default or a decree may be entered.

4. Your written response to the summons and petition must be on form WPF DR 01.0300, Response to Petition (Domestic Relations). Information about how to get this form may be obtained by contacting the clerk of the court, by contacting the Office of the Administrator for the Courts at (360) 705-5328, or from the Internet at the Washington State Courts homepage:

    http://www.courts.wa.gov/forms

5. If you wish to seek the advice of an attorney in this matter, you should do so promptly so that your written response, if any, may be served on time.

6. One method of serving a copy of your response on the petitioner is to send it by certified mail with return receipt requested.

7. Other:

This summons is issued pursuant to RCW 4.28.100 and Superior Court Civil Rule 4.1 of the state of Washington.

Dated: March 30, 200-

Sue Snoopie
Signature of Lawyer or Petitioner

SUE SNOOPIE
Print or Type Name

FILE ORIGINAL OF YOUR RESPONSE
WITH THE CLERK OF THE COURT AT:

SERVE A COPY OF YOUR RESPONSE ON:

[X] Petitioner [You may list an address that is not your residential address where you agree to accept legal documents.]

[ ] Petitioner's Lawyer

SPOKANE SUPERIOR COURT
[Name of Court]

SUE SNOOPIE
[Name]

NORTH 123 BEAGLE STREET
[Address]

[Address]

SPOKANE, WASHINGTON 99201

SUMMONS BY PUBLICATION (SMPB) - Page 2 of 2
WPF DR 01.0270 (9/2001) - RCW 4.28.100; CR 4.1

SELF-COUNSEL PRESS – DIV WA (15-2) 01

SAMPLE 33
MOTION AND DECLARATION TO SERVE BY MAIL

SUPERIOR COURT OF WASHINGTON
COUNTY OF SPOKANE

In re the Marriage of:

SUE SNOOPIE

                                   Petitioner,

and

SAM SNOOPIE

                                 Respondent.

NO. XX-X-XXXXX-X

MOTION AND DECLARATION
TO SERVE BY MAIL
(MTAF)

I. MOTION

___SUE SNOOPIE_____ [moving party] moves the court for an order allowing service of the summons and petition by mail.

Dated: ___MARCH 30, 200-_____   *Sue Snoopie*
                                       Signature of Lawyer or Moving Party

                                     ___SUE SNOOPIE_____
                                       Print or Type Name

II. DECLARATION

2.1.   Service should be made by mail because:

      [ ]   _____ [nonmoving party] is not a resident of this state.
      [ ]   _____ [nonmoving party] cannot be found in this state.
      [X]   the moving party is proceeding in forma pauperis and cannot afford service by publication or personal service.

2.2   The moving party has not been able to locate or serve the nonmoving party because:

      [ ]   the nonmoving party has departed from Washington to avoid service of summons.
      [X]   the nonmoving party has concealed himself/herself to avoid service of summons.
      [ ]   other:

SAMPLE 33—Continued

2.3 The facts supporting the above allegations are:
I have not been able to locate the Respondent, even through
the Respondent's employer, family, and friends.

2.4 The following efforts were made to locate the nonmoving party for personal service:
I have contacted his emplyer, XYZ Corp., and Emily Snoopy,
John Jackson, and Bob Sneaky, none of whom had any
information regarding the Respondent's whereabouts.

2.5 Service by mail is as likely to provide actual notice as service by publication.

2.6 The mailings should be sent to the following address:

6000 East 6000 - 14th Ave., Yakima, WA 98083

2.7 This address is:

[ ] The last known mailing address of the nonmoving party.
[X] The mailing address of the nonmoving party's parent or nearest living relative.
[ ] Other:

2.8 Other:

I declare under penalty of perjury under the laws of the state of Washington that the foregoing is true and correct.

Signed at SPOKANE, WASHINGTON   on MARCH 30, 200- .
      [Place]   [Date]

Sue Snoopie
Signature of Moving Party

SUE SNOOPIE
Print or Type Name

SAMPLE 34
ORDER ALLOWING SERVICE BY MAIL

SUPERIOR COURT OF WASHINGTON
COUNTY OF SPOKANE

In re the Marriage of:

SUE SNOOPIE

Petitioner,

and

SAM SNOOPIE

Respondent.

NO. XX-X-XXXXX-X

ORDER ALLOWING SERVICE
BY MAIL
(ORRSR)

I. BASIS

The court has considered SUE SNOOPIE [moving party]'s motion and declaration requesting an order allowing service of the summons and petition by mail.

II. FINDINGS

Based on the motion and declaration, the court FINDS that the summons and petition in this matter should be served on SAM SNOOPIE [nonmoving party] by mail in accordance with CR 4(d)(4).

III. ORDER

IT IS ORDERED:

3.1   The summons and petition shall be served on the nonmoving party by mail by a person 18 years of age or over and competent to be a witness but not the moving party.

3.2   Two (2) copies shall be mailed postage prepaid, one by ordinary first class mail, and the other by certified mail, return receipt requested, showing when, and to whom, delivered, each showing a return address for the sender or an address through which correspondence may be directed to the sender.

3.3   The mailings shall be sent to the following address(es):

East 6000 - 14th Avenue, Yakima, WA 98093

ORD ALLOWING SERV BY MAIL (ORRSR) - Page 1 of 2
WPF DR 01.0285 (9/2001) - RCW 4.28.100; CR 4 (d)(4)

SELF-COUNSEL PRESS – DIV WA (17-1) 01

3.4   These addresses are:

        [X]   The last known mailing address of the nonmoving party.
        [ ]   The mailing address of the nonmoving party's parent or nearest living relative.
        [ ]   Other:

3.5   A summons and petition mailed to the nonmoving party in care of parents or other individuals shall be addressed directly to the parent or other individual with a note enclosed asking that the summons and petition be delivered to the nonmoving party.

3.6   The person mailing the summons and petition shall complete a Return of Service form.

Dated: __March 30, 200-_____   *J.M Judge*_____
                                                              Judge/Commissioner

Presented by:

*Sue Snoopie*_____
Signature

__SUE SNOOPIE_____
Print or Type Name

SUPERIOR COURT OF WASHINGTON
COUNTY OF   SPOKANE

In re the Marriage of:

SUE SNOOPIE

                                 Petitioner,

and

SAM SNOOPIE

                                 Respondent.

NO. XX-X-XXXXX-X

SUMMONS BY MAIL
(SM)

TO THE RESPONDENT:

1.   The petitioner has started an action in the above court requesting:

        [X]   that your marriage be dissolved.
        [ ]   a legal separation.
        [ ]   that the validity of your marriage be determined.

    Additional requests, if any, are stated in the petition, a copy of which is attached.

2.   You must respond to this summons by serving a copy of your written response on the person signing this summons and by filing the original with the clerk of the court. If you do not serve your written response within 90 days from the date of mailing of this summons (90 days after the 30th day of _____March_____, 200-), the court may enter an order of default against you, and the court may, without further notice to you, enter a decree and approve or provide for other relief requested in the petition. In the case of a dissolution of marriage, the court will not enter the final decree until at least 90 days after service and filing. If you serve a notice of appearance on the undersigned person, you are entitled to notice before an order of default or a decree may be entered.

3.   Your written response to the summons and petition must be on form WPF DR 01.0300, Response to Petition (Domestic Relations). Information about how to get this form may be obtained by contacting the clerk of the court, by contacting the Office of the Administrator for the Courts at (360) 705-5328, or from the Internet at the Washington State Courts homepage:

                http://www.courts.wa.gov/forms

4.   If this action has not been filed with the court, you may demand that the petitioner file this action with the court. If you do so, the demand must be in writing and must be served upon the person publishing this summons. Within 14 days after you serve the demand, the petitioner must file this action with the court, or the service on you of this summons will be void.

SUMMONS BY MAIL (SM) - Page 1 of 2
WPF DR 01.0290 (9/2001) - RCW 4.28.100; CR 4 (d)(4); CR 4.1

SELF-COUNSEL PRESS – DIV WA (18-1) 01

5.   If you wish to seek the advice of an attorney in this matter, you should do so promptly so that your written response, if any, may be served on time.

6.   One method of serving a copy of your response on the petitioner is to send it by certified mail with return receipt requested.

This summons is issued pursuant to RCW 4.28.100 and Superior Court Civil Rule 4.1 of the state of Washington.

Dated: March 30, 200-

Sue Snoopie
Signature of Lawyer or Petitioner

SUE SNOOPIE
Print or Type Name

FILE ORIGINAL OF YOUR RESPONSE
WITH THE CLERK OF THE COURT AT:

SERVE A COPY OF YOUR RESPONSE ON:

[X] Petitioner [You may list an address that is not your residential address where you agree to accept legal documents.]

[ ] Petitioner's Lawyer

SPOKANE SUPERIOR COURT
[Name of Court]

SUE SNOOPIE
[Name]

[Address]

NORTH 123 BEAGLE STREET
[Address]

SPOKANE, WA 99201

Date Mailed: March 30, 200-

NOTICE OF TAKING DEFAULT AND ENTRY OF DECREE OF DISSOLUTION AFTER ONE YEAR

**SUPERIOR COURT OF WASHINGTON
FOR COUNTY OF   SPOKANE**

In Re the Marriage of:

    SUE SNOOPIE

                        Petitioner

and

    SAM SNOOPIE

                        Respondent

NO: 8800000

**NOTICE OF TAKING DEFAULT
AND ENTRY OF DECREE OF
DISSOLUTION AFTER ONE YEAR**

TO: SAM SNOOPIE   , Respondent, above named.

YOU ARE HEREBY NOTIFIED that more than ten (10) days from the date you receive this notice, on the 24th day of January, 200– ,* by certified mail or in person, I will present to the Superior Court of the state of Washington in and for the County of Spokane , an Order of Default, Conclusions of Law, Findings of Fact and Decree of Dissolution (divorce) for entry by said court. Said proposed Decree that I will present for entry will follow the request of the Petition herein.

This notice is in compliance with Rule 55f(1)(B) for the Superior Court of the state of Washington. This notice is sent to you by certified mail, return receipt requested, and the return receipt has been filed with the clerk of the court.

Done this 10th day of January , 200– .

                              IN PERSON

                              Sue Snoopie

                              (signature of petitioner)

*This date must be at least 13 days after the day you mailed it.

SUPERIOR COURT OF WASHINGTON
FOR COUNTY OF   SPOKANE

In Re the Marriage of:

SUE SNOOPIE

                                        Petitioner

and

SAM SNOOPIE

                                        Respondent

NO: 8800000

DECLARATION OF MAILING
(NOTICE OF TAKING DEFAULT AND
ENTRY OF DECREE OF DISSOLUTION)

The undersigned declares under penalty of perjury under the laws of the state of Washington that the following is true: ~~he~~ (she) is the petitioner, herein. That ~~he~~ (she) placed in the United States mails an envelope(s) with a certified mail receipt attached; together with correct postage affixed, addressed to the respondent at the following last known address(~~es~~):

Sam Snoopie East 600000 - 14th Avenue Yakima, Washington 98093

Said envelope(s) contained a certified copy of the Notice of Taking Default and Entry of Decree of Dissolution, when more than one year has elapsed after the start of this proceeding.

[X] A return receipt was received back from the Post Office Department bearing the signature of the respondent. Said receipt is attached to this declaration in support of the taking of default and entry of Decree of Dissolution, herein.

[ ] The mailed envelope(s) was (were) returned by the Post Office Department indicating that the Post Office Department was unable to deliver the envelope(s) to the respondent. The petitioner has also given Notice of Taking Default and Entry of Decree Dissolution by one publication in a newspaper of general circulation in this county. A copy of the newspaper's affidavit concerning said publication is attached hereto.

Sue Snoopie
(signature of petitioner)

MOTION FOR NON-SUIT AND ORDER OF DISMISSAL

SUPERIOR COURT OF WASHINGTON
FOR COUNTY OF   SPOKANE

In Re the Marriage of:

SUE SNOOPIE

                Petitioner

and

SAM SNOOPIE

                Respondent

NO: __8800000__

MOTION FOR NON-SUIT AND
ORDER OF DISMISSAL

MOTION

Comes now the Petitioner, above-named, stating that ~~he~~ (she) no longer wishes to terminate their marriage and, therefore, moves for Non-Suit and Order of Dismissal.

Sam Snoopie
Respondent — In Person

Sue Snoopie
Petitioner — In Person

ORDER

Upon presentation of the above Motion for Non-Suit Order of Dismissal, the court having examined the court file in this matter and being fully advised in the premises, it is by the court ORDERED, that said motion be and the same is hereby granted. THIS CASE IS DISMISSED.

Done in open court this __10th__ day of __January__, 200– .

I.M. Commissioner
Judge/Court Commissioner

Presented by:

Sue Snoopie
Petitioner — In Person

MOTION AND DECLARATION FOR ORDER TO COMMENCE AND PROSECUTE PROCEEDING IN FORMA PAUPERIS

SUPERIOR COURT OF WASHINGTON
FOR COUNTY OF   SPOKANE

In Re the Marriage of:

    SUE SNOOPIE

                    Petitioner

and

    SAM SNOOPIE

                    Respondent

NO: 8800000

MOTION AND DECLARATION FOR ORDER TO COMMENCE AND PROSECUTE PROCEEDING IN FORMA PAUPERIS

MOTION

COMES NOW the Petitioner and moves the court for an order authorizing:

[✗]   to be authorized to file this petition in forma pauperis.

This motion is based on the following declaration of the petitioner.

Dated this 5th day of ___December___ , 200– .

Sue Snoopie
Petitioner

    SUE SNOOPIE   , declares under penalty of perjury under the laws of the state of Washington that the following is true and correct.

I.

I am one of the parties in the above-entitled proceeding. My marriage to SAM SNOOPIE is irretrievably broken. We are at this time unable to live together as married persons. This proceeding to terminate our marriage is brought in good faith and it is my present intention to proceed to a final dissolution of our marriage.

II.

I bring this proceeding in person, without an attorney, because I lack financial means to pay legal counsel. I cannot, without financial hardship, pay to the clerk of this court the statutory fee for filing my Petition. I also do not have the funds to pay a process server to serve the documents.

WHEREFORE, I request the court for:

(1)   [X]   An order allowing commencement and prosecution of this proceeding In Forma Pauperis;

(2)   [X]   An order directing the clerk of this court to file and issue my Petition or any other papers herein without any fee, cost or charge whatsoever;

Dated in Washington this 5th day of December , 200–

Sue Snoopie
Petitioner's Signature

SUPERIOR COURT OF WASHINGTON
FOR COUNTY OF   SPOKANE

In Re the Marriage of:		
SUE SNOOPIE		NO: __8800000__
	Petitioner	ORDER AUTHORIZING
and		PROCEEDING IN FORMA
		PAUPERIS
SAM SNOOPIE		
	Respondent	

The Petitioner, above named, having presented to the court a sufficient declaration to proceed In Forma Pauperis and the court being of the opinion that the order asked for should issue, NOW, THERFORE,

[**✗**]   IT IS HEREBY ORDERED, ADJUDGED AND DECREED that the parties are hereby authorized to prosecute this action In Forma Pauperis; and the clerk of this court is ordered and directed to file and issue papers and pleadings as requested by either party without prepayment of any fee, cost or charge whatsoever. In approving this order, the court reserves the right to review this authorization and require the payment of the fee if justified at the time of final hearing.

Done in OPEN COURT this __5th__ day of _____January_____, _200–_ .

I.M. Commissioner
Judge/Court Commissioner

Presented by:

Sue Snoopie
In Person

SAMPLE 41
DECLARATION OF MAILING

IN THE SUPERIOR COURT OF WASHINGTON
FOR COUNTY OF   SPOKANE

In Re the Marriage of:

SUE SNOOPIE

                 Petitioner

and

SAM SNOOPIE

                 Respondent

NO: 8800000

DECLARATION OF MAILING

The undersigned declares under penalty of perjury under the laws of the state of Washington that the following is true: ~~he~~ (she) is the petitioner herein. That ~~he~~ (she) placed in the United States mails an envelope(s) with a certified mail receipt attached; together with correct postagte affixed, addressed to the respondent at the following last known address:

Sam Snoopie East 60000 - 14th Avenue, Yakima, Washington, 98093

Said envelope(s) contained a copy of each of the following documents:

Summons Petition

[**✗**]   A return receipt was received back from the Post Office Department bearing the signature of the respondent. Said receipt is attached to this declaration in support of the taking of default and entry of Decree of Dissolution, herein.

Sue Snoopie
Petitioner's Signature

APPENDIX
A CHECKLIST OF STEPS TO TAKE

These lists summarize the steps that will need to be followed whether you obtain your own divorce or have an attorney handle your case. This summary can serve as a checklist. Be sure that you understand the details of each of the procedures as explained in this book.

a. IF YOU AND YOUR SPOUSE BOTH SIGN THE PETITION

1. Fill out the Petition and sign.

2. Have your spouse fill out and sign the Acceptance of Service/Joinder.

3. File the Petition with county clerk.

4. Wait 90 days.

5. Fill out the Decree of Dissolution (divorce) and the Findings of Fact and Conclusions of Law, Parenting Plan, and Order of Child Support.

6. Go to court for the hearing and have the Decree of Dissolution (divorce) signed by the judge or court commissioner.

7. You are then divorced.

b. IF YOUR SPOUSE IS NOT COOPERATING, OR OBJECTS TO YOUR TERMS

1. Fill out the Petition and Summons.

2. File the Petition and Summons with the county clerk.

3. Have a copy of the Petition and Summons served on your spouse.

4. After your spouse is served, file the Return of Service with the county clerk.

5. Wait 90 days after the date your spouse is served.

6. If your spouse has objected and an attorney has filed such objection with the county clerk, find an attorney to represent you.

7. If no objection has been filed within 90 days, fill out the Findings of Fact and the Decree of Dissolution (divorce), Parenting Plan, and Order of Child Support.

8. Go to court for the hearing and have the Decree of Dissolution (divorce) signed by the judge or court commissioner.

9. You are then divorced.

c. IF YOUR SPOUSE IS MISSING

1. Fill out the Petition, the Summons, and the Declaration of Service of Summons by Publication.

153

2. File the Petition, the Summons, and the Declaration of Service of Summons by Publication with county clerk.

3. Fill out the Summons by Publication.

4. Take the Summons to a newspaper for publication once a week for six consecutive weeks.

5. File the Declaration of Publication with the county clerk.

6. Wait 90 days after the date of the first publication of the Summons.

7. If your spouse has objected and an attorney has filed such objection with the county clerk, find an attorney to represent you.

8. If no objection has been filed within 90 days, fill out the Findings of Fact and the Decree of Dissolution (divorce), Parenting Plan, and Order of Child Support.

9. Go to court for the hearing and have the Decree of Dissolution (divorce) signed by the judge or court commissioner.

10. You are then divorced.

GLOSSARY

ACKNOWLEDGE
The signature and seal of a notary public

ACTION
The suit for dissolution of marriage that a person brings to end his or her marriage

ADVERTISING
In this context, a legal notice published in a newspaper

AFFIDAVIT
A written statement signed in front of a notary public and witnessed by the notary

AMEND
The addition of words to a paper that is filed with the county clerk concerning a dissolution of marriage

ANNULMENT
The termination of an illegal marriage, called "declaration of invalidity" in Washington's divorce act

APPEAL
To ask a higher court to decide if the dissolution is proper and legal

APPEARANCE
The filing of a paper with the county clerk contesting the dissolution and refusing the requests of the petitioner

BAILIFF
The judge's assistant in court

BENCH
The judge or court commissioner's seat in the courtroom

CASE NUMBER
A number that is placed on the Petition when it is filed. The same number is used on all other papers filed in the same action.

CERTIFIED COPY
A copy of something that the county clerk places a seal on and states that the copy is the same as the original in the court file

CONTEMPT OF COURT
The failure to do something the court has ordered

CONTESTED DIVORCE
When the respondent does not agree with the claims and requests of the Petition and files a paper with the county clerk stating his or her objections

COOPERATIVE
When both spouses want the divorce and agree with the requests in the Petition

COUNTY ASSESSOR
An elected public official at the county courthouse who will provide the legal description of real estate if given the street address

COUNTY CLERK
An elected public official who keeps the court records and with whom dissolution papers are filed at the county courthouse

COURT COMMISSIONER
A person appointed by the court to sign dissolution papers on behalf of a judge

DECISION
The ruling of the judge or court commissioner when the spouses do not agree

DECREE OF DISSOLUTION
The paper that dissolves a marriage when signed by a judge or court commissioner

DECREE OF SEPARATE MAINTE-NANCE
A paper signed by the judge or court commissioner that keeps a couple married, but living separate and apart

DEED
A legal paper transferring ownership of real estate from seller to buyer

DEFAULT
When the respondent fails to file a paper objecting to what was asked for in the Petition for Dissolution

DEFAULT DIVORCE CALENDAR
A list of the divorce cases to be heard by the judge or court commissioner on a certain day, also called a "Default Divorce Docket"

ENCUMBRANCE
The unpaid balance due on a house or any other property

EQUITY
The duty a judge or court commissioner has to be fair to both parties; also the value of a house or other property less balance due on the purchase price

FEES
Payment to the county clerk for filing a Petition; also the wages paid to an attorney, a sheriff, or a process server

"FILED" STAMP
The stamp the county clerk uses on copies of papers submitted to show the date they are filed with the county clerk

HARASSMENT
Annoying or threatening to harm someone or his or her children or property

INDIGENT
Having money for living expenses only with nothing left over

IN FORMA PAUPERIS
A legal term for asking the court to waive your filing fees

JUDGMENT
The decision of the judge or court commission; it is a part of the Decree of Dissolution

LEGAL DESCRIPTION
The description of the location of real estate which differs from the street address

LEGAL NOTICES
Publication in a weekly newspaper in the classified ad section, giving notice of a court proceeding

LEGAL SERVICES OFFICE
An attorney's office that gives free legal help to eligible clients

LITIGANT
A person in a lawsuit; a petitioner is a litigant

MAINTENANCE
The money paid by one spouse to another after the divorce; formerly called "alimony"

MODIFY
To change the custody or support of a child after the Decree of Dissolution has been signed by the judge or court commissioner

MOTION
A request to the court asking that something be done, such as issuing a Restraining Order

NONSUPPORT
The failure of a person to support his or her family

NOTARY PUBLIC
Someone appointed by the governor of the state of Washington, before whom you sign your papers, if required; notaries work at banks, real estate offices, and insurance companies

OATH
To make a statement in which one promises to tell the truth to the judge or court commissioner

PETITION
The paper requesting a dissolution of marriage; it is filed at the county clerk's office

PETITIONER
The person asking the court for a dissolution of marriage

PLEADING
Any paper in the court file concerning a dissolution

PROCESS
The delivery of papers to the appropriate person and the sworn statement of the person who delivered the papers that they have been delivered

PROCESS SERVER
The person who delivers papers and makes a sworn statement that they were delivered properly

PROPERTY SETTLEMENT AGREEMENT
A written contract betwen two spouses agreeing to a division of property and debts, and custody and support of the children

PUBLISH
Placement of a legal notice in a weekly newspaper

R.C.W.
Revised Code of Washington; Washington state laws

RECONCILED
To resume living together as husband and wife

RECONCILIATION PERIOD
The 90-day waiting period from the time that the Petition is given to the county clerk and a copy of the Petition is sent to the respondent spouse to the time the judge or court commissioner grants the dissolution

RESPONDENT
The spouse who is not filing the Petition of Dissolution

RESTRAINING ORDER
A paper signed by a judge or court commissioner that prohibits a person from doing somehing or orders a person to do something